KNOW ME

D1477969

Know Me

A Pocket Guide to
Daily Scriptural Prayer

David E. Rosage

Servant Publications
Ann Arbor, Michigan

Published by Servant Publications
P.O. Box 8617
Ann Arbor, Michigan 48107

Cover design by Michael Andaloro
Cover photo © 1990 The Stock Market/ Kunio Owaki

91 92 93 94 95   10 9 8 7 6 5 4 3 2 1

Printed in the United States of America
ISBN 0-89283-693-8

Library of Congress-in-Publication Data

Rosage, David E.
    Know me : a pocket guide to daily scriptural
prayer / Dvid E. Rosage.
        p.   cm.
ISBN 0-89283-693-8
    1. Devotional calendars—Catholic Church.
    2. Bible—Meditations.   I. Title.
BX2182.2.R65 1991
242'.2—dc20   91-6861

In Gratitude

With St. Paul I pray:
*"I give thanks to my God every time
I think of you . . ."*

To My Many Dedicated Friends,
especially
Mary Krone and Joan Thielen,
whose indefatigable and persevering
efforts have contributed immensely
in bringing this work to completion.

*May the fruits of your labors bring all of you
abundant blessings!*

Contents

Introduction

In the name of the Father,
and of the Son,
and of the Holy Spirit. Amen.

WITH THIS TRINITARIAN INVOCATION, we introduce this selection of daily reflections as a scriptural pathway leading us to a deeper knowledge of the presence and power of the Triune God in our lives. This is the one God who has revealed himself in three Divine Persons as Father, Son, and Holy Spirit. This is the one God who has created us, redeemed us, and sanctified us—pointing our lives toward eternity.

WE STAND IN NEED

Life on this planet is only a period of probation, a time of preparation for that eternal bliss which is our final destiny. According to God's inscrutable design, the best way to prepare is to give ourselves totally and exclusively to him as we go about our daily round of duties. When we make this daily offering of our lives, we enable the Lord to transform each of us into the person he wants us to be. That daily oblation of self and our consequent transformation completes God's plan in preparing each of us for our heavenly home as a member of the Trinitarian family.

We are painfully aware that we cannot fulfill this wonderful plan on our own resources, sincere as our efforts may be. If we are to journey heavenward, we need divine assistance every step of the way. We need hope and inspiration, motivation and encouragement, support and nourishment. We also need constant guidance, lest we veer off the path God has set before us.

All the assistance we need has been provided by the Holy Trinity. Each of the three Divine Persons is eager to meet our particular needs if we will only humbly seek his divine help. We attribute to each person of the Trinity a particular ministry in salvation history, yet each person in the Godhead acts in concert to supply the gifts and graces that we require for the journey. The Father is Creator; the Son, our Savior and Redeemer; the Holy Spirit, the Paraclete and Comforter.

DAY BY DAY KNOWING HIM BETTER

This volume offers a convenient compendium of scriptural passages and commentary for a year of daily prayer and reflection that build our knowledge of the Father, Son, and Holy Spirit. It is the fourth in a series of pocket guides that include *Follow Me, Abide in Me,* and *Rejoice in Me.*

Under twelve different headings, one for each month of the year, thirty-one scriptural passages and accompanying commentary are provided for each day of the month. For the first ten days, we recall the creative and providential role of the Father in the economy of salvation; the next ten days recount the redemptive love of Jesus; days twenty-one through thirty are devoted to the Holy Spirit's work of sanctification. Day thirty-one reminds us of the shared ministry of all three persons in the Holy Trinity as the one, undivided God.

To sum up this shared ministry and unity, a slightly different arrangement is followed in the last month. Once again ten days are devoted to each person of the Trinity, but the emphasis throughout is on how each of the three persons in the Godhead acts in concert in the Eucharistic celebration— drawing all of us in the body of Christ into unity with God and one another.

The brief commentary or reflection after each daily scriptural passage is meant to lead us into a quiet prayer posture so that we can listen to the Lord with our whole being. It should lead us into a personal prayer encounter with the Lord himself. For some Scriptures, your own personal reflections may be even more effective in leading you into a time of prayer.

A METHOD FOR PRAYER

Like the other titles in this series of pocket books for daily scriptural prayer, *Know Me* suggests a method of prayer for those who desire a more personal relationship with the Lord, but think they do not have time for prayer. Here are a few directives:

1. Before retiring at night select a short Scripture passage from those suggested, preferably following the order in which they are listed. One verse, one phrase, or even one word may be sufficient. Read it slowly and let every word sink into your heart.

Try to relax for a few moments and ponder the message you have just heard. As you listen to God's Word, your attitude must be "Lord, I know you are present here in your Word; what are you saying to me here and now?"

The import of the message will implant itself in your subconscious and remain with you throughout the night. If you wake during the night or when you awaken in the morning, the thought may well be uppermost in your mind. Even if it does not penetrate into your consciousness, its formative power is at work in your heart.

2. Reread the passage in the morning and listen at the core of your being to what the Lord may be saying to you. Spend some time reflecting on his Word, or just basking in his presence and being warmed by his love.

3. If a certain thought strikes you, you may want to linger with it for some time. Jotting down an insight or thought in a journal will assist you in growing and maturing in your relationship with the Lord.

4. Throughout the day recall the thought, the inspiration, or the message which seemed to speak to you. Perhaps making a note of a word or phrase on a slip of paper and keeping it in your pocket or displaying it in a strategic spot (where you will see it often during the course of the day) may help you recall the presence of the Lord and his message.

5. On some days you may not have experienced any great insights or illumination from the passage. This is no reason to be discouraged. The Word of the Lord will mold and transform your heart without you even being aware of it. For example, if you are inclined to be impatient, and if the message of Scripture pointed to the patience

of Jesus in dealing with his disciples, his enemies, or sinners, you will automatically be more patient throughout the day and wonder whether you are being transformed. But you cannot possibly be aware of the number of times you were more patient than usual. That is known to God alone. He does not want us to be spiritual accountants.

FRUITS OF THIS APPROACH

Fidelity to a daily prayer practice will eventually bear much fruit, even though at present we may not be conscious that anything is taking place within us. As noted, the fruit of this kind of prayer does not always register intellectually, because such prayer influences and transforms our heart, attitude, and actions.

This kind of prayer is sometimes called contemplative prayer or prayer of the heart. It will enable us to know each person of the Blessed Trinity in a deeper, more personal way. This kind of heart knowledge will increase our love for each of the three Divine Persons in God, since we can only love those persons we know, those to whom we have listened, and those with whom we have shared our lives.

This introduction began with an invocation addressed to the Holy Trinity, and it concludes with a brief hymn of praise to the Father, Son, and Holy Spirit:

Glory be to the Father,
and to the Son,
and to the Holy Spirit,
as it was in the beginning,
is now, and ever shall be,
world without end. Amen.

Meeting the Father, Son, and Holy Spirit in the Old Testament

"Now this is eternal life, that they should know you, the only true God, and the one whom you sent, Jesus Christ." (Jn 17:3)

FATHER

1 *"I, the LORD, am your God, who brought you out of the land of Egypt, that place of slavery. You shall not have other gods besides me."*

(Dt 5:6-7)

The Israelites turned away from the one true God to worship the false gods of the pagans. As a gracious Father, he sent prophets to persuade them to return to him. When this failed, the Lord had to use some drastic measure to bring them back to him.

In today's crisis in faith people are worshiping the false gods of wealth, power, prestige, pleasure. We need to ask ourselves if there are any plastic or neon gods in our lives.

Listen to the Lord's plea: "Come back to me with all your heart."

2 *"Hear, O Israel! The LORD is our God, the LORD alone! Therefore, you shall love the LORD, your God, with all your heart, and with all your soul, and with all your strength."* (Dt 6:4-5)

The devout Jew was to wear this *shema* as a pendant on his arm and forehead and inscribe it on the doorposts and gates of his home. This would remind him that God was to be the number one priority in his life.

As Christians our privilege is far greater. The Lord himself dwells with us and within us, and writes his law on our hearts.

Lord, keep us always aware that our life must be totally dedicated to you.

3 *Here comes with power the Lord GOD, / who rules by his strong arm.* (Is 40:10)

The power of God is the mightiest ever, because it is the power of love. His love for each one of us is absolutely infinite, unconditional, enduring. Love by its very nature requires a response, otherwise it is a rejected love.

Our response is to do everything throughout the day to please him. The object of love is always to please the beloved.

4 *You will show me the path to life, / fullness of joys in your presence, / the delights at your right hand forever.* (Ps 16:11)

When we permit the Lord to take us by the hand and lead us along the path that he has mapped out for us, we shall experience the joys which only he can give.

If we truly love the Lord, we will want to follow all his directives. Our obedience is not only a means of achieving our eternal destiny, but a love-offering to please our gracious Father. Then our heart will be filled with delight at his right hand forever.

5 *When you pass through the water, / I will be with you; / in the rivers you shall not drown. / When you walk through fire, you shall not be burned; / the flames shall not consume you.*

(Is 43:2)

Since our gracious Father freed us from the slavery of sin and its dreadful consequences, we do belong to him and are deeply indebted to him.

We are grateful, too, that he loves us so much and calls us by name. We are flattered when someone calls us by name. How much more gratifying knowing that the Lord knows us by name.

Father, I thank you.

6 *"Your strength is not in numbers, nor does your power depend upon stalwart men; but you are the God of the lowly, the helper of the oppressed, the supporter of the weak, the protector of the forsaken, the savior of those without hope."*

(Jdt 9:11)

This prayer of Judith is a reminder to us that God is our protector also. He comes to our rescue more frequently than we will ever know. Our Father is greatly pleased when we place our trust and confidence in him.

The Lord heard the prayer of Judith and spared her and her people. His power, prompted by his infinite love, is by no means curtailed in guiding and protecting us. He wants us to implore his help with confidence and trust at all times.

7 *I love you, O LORD, my strength, / O LORD, my rock, my fortress, my deliverer. / My God, my rock of refuge, / my shield, the horn of my salvation, my stronghold!* (Ps 18:2-3)

The psalmist's expression of love for the Lord for all that the Lord has done for him, enkindles within us a deeper appreciation of the Lord's protective love. His love overshadows us at every moment without our even being consciously aware of his abiding presence.

This kind of love generates confidence and trust. Father, grant me the grace to trust you always, everywhere and in all circumstances.

8 *... The LORD is the eternal God, / creator of the ends of the earth. / He does not faint nor grow weary, / and his knowledge is beyond scrutiny. / He gives strength to the fainting; / for the weak he makes vigor abound.* (Is 40:28-29) /

God did not merely create our world and then leave it on its own. On the contrary, he continues to energize and sustain it at every moment.

He creates new life at conception, gives seed the potential to reproduce, replenishes our water supply, restores fertility to a harvested field. He mends broken bones and heals wounds.

His constant presence and power are manifestations of his overwhelming love for each one of us.

9 *The LORD is my shepherd; I shall not want. / In verdant pastures he gives me repose; / Beside restful waters he leads me; / he refreshes my soul.* (Ps 23:1-2)

We often pray this psalm because we find great comfort and reassurance in it. The psalmist tries to describe in pastoral imagery the boundless loving care which the Lord has for each one of us.

As a solicitous Shepherd, he protects us with his rod and guides us with his staff. He leads us safely through the dark valleys of our life. The table he spreads before us is a symbol of the gift of himself in the Eucharistic banquet.

Pray this psalm frequently and fervently.

10 *Give thanks to the LORD, / for he is good, / for his mercy endures forever; . . . / Give thanks to the God of heaven, / for his mercy endures forever.* (Ps 136:1, 26)

The twenty-six repetitions of the refrain "for his mercy endures forever" identify our God as a merciful, compassionate, forgiving, healing Father. It leaves no doubt about the intensity of his unconditional love for us. He wants to forgive and heal us even more than we desire it for ourselves.

With humble, grateful hearts, we need to be open to receive his mercy.

Let us "Give thanks to the God of heaven, for his mercy endures forever."

SON

11 *"I will put enmity between you and the woman, / and between your offspring and hers; / He will strike at your head, / while you strike at his heel."* (Gn 3:15)

This is the very first prophecy promising a Redeemer to restore our fragmented relationship with our compassionate Father. It gives us a hint about the future Incarnation of Jesus into our world as our Redeemer. St. John writes: ". . . The Son of God was revealed to destroy the works of the devil" (1 Jn 3:8).

Prayerfully ponder the tremendous condescension of the Lord of heaven and earth who loved us so much that he gave us his only Son.

12 *Therefore, thus says the Lord GOD: / See, I am laying a stone in Zion, / a stone that has been tested, / A precious cornerstone as a sure foundation; / he who puts his faith in it shall not be shaken.* (Is 28:16)

Even though the Father, through the prophets, had prepared his people for the coming of the Messiah, they rejected him as the cornerstone.

Jesus challenges us to live his way of life, not only as the cornerstone, but the whole foundation of our temporal happiness, which is the prelude of the eternal bliss of heaven.

Pray daily for those who have rejected him and also for those who have not yet recognized him as the cornerstone.

13 *But a shoot shall sprout from the stump of Jesse, and from his roots a bud shall blossom.* (Is 11:1)

In his loving concern the Father reaffirmed again and again the promise of the Messiah and foretold many details about his reign. Lineage was very important to the Hebrews; hence, God revealed details about who the royal ancestors of Jesus would be.

As the adopted children of God we are members of his royal family, sisters and brothers to Jesus. We are destined to be united with this royal family in heaven for all eternity to sing God's praises. We are special; we are privileged.

14 *... The virgin shall be with child, and bear a son, and shall name him Immanuel.*
(Is 7:14)

Jesus fulfilled this prophecy eight hundred years later when he rose from the dead so that he might abide with us and within us in his risen, exalted, glorified life and love. He is Emmanuel—"God is with us" (Mt 1:23).

His abiding presence also fulfills his promise: ". . . Behold, I am with you always, until the end of the age" (Mt 28:20).

When his death was imminent, he assured us: "I will not leave you orphans; I will come to you" (Jn 14:18). Our Emmanuel is with us always.

15 *Fairer in beauty are you than the sons of men; / grace is poured out upon your lips; thus God has blessed you forever.* (Ps 45:3)

The image of marriage is used in the Old Testament to portray the close bond between God and his people. Yahweh is the bridegroom; Israel the bride.

In prophecy, this same image prepares the way for a deep, personal union between Jesus and his bride, the members of his body, the church. Jesus is dwelling with us and within us in his glorified life.

Lord Jesus, increase in us an ardent desire to live more closely with you, since you are dwelling within us.

16 *He shall govern your people with justice / and your afflicted ones with judgment. / The mountains shall yield peace for the people, / and the hills justice.* (Ps 72:2-3)

The many prophecies about the coming of the Messiah brought great hope and joy to the people of the Old Testament. They were always in conflict with their pagan neighbors. They longed for peace.

Jesus showed us the way to peace and justice when he proclaimed the law of love and laid down the guidelines of that law in the Beatitudes. Jesus lived the Beatitudes as much as he taught them.

Let us pause to recall and be grateful how privileged a people we are to know the ways of peace and justice and to enjoy all the fruits of redemption.

17 *". . . You are a priest forever, according to the order of Melchizedek."* (Ps 110:4)

In the eternal now of God there is no time or space. Jesus is continually offering his redemptive sacrifice to praise and glorify his Father.

When we offer the Eucharistic Sacrifice, we are privileged to join Jesus and all the hosts of heaven and earth in this unending sacrifice to worship, praise, and thank our loving Father.

Jesus, help us to appreciate more deeply this tremendous mystery of faith!

18 *Rejoice heartily, O daughter Zion, / shout for joy, O daughter Jerusalem! / See, your king shall come to you; / a just savior is he, / Meek, and riding on an ass . . .* (Zec 9:9)

The Messiah and King will not come as a great political leader, nor as a conquering warrior, but he will come "meek and riding on an ass." This animal, a humble beast of burden, was the hallmark of Jesus as he sojourned here on earth.

As disciples, we are called to cultivate the mind and heart of our Master. Jesus bade us: "Learn from me, for I am meek and humble of heart" (Mt 11:29).

Lord, show us how to become meek and humble of heart.

19 *Though he was harshly treated, he submitted / and opened not his mouth; / Like a lamb led to the slaughter / or a sheep before the shearers, / he was silent and opened not his mouth.*
(Is 53:7)

Jesus proved himself to be the true Lamb of God when he willingly and silently laid down his life for us. He assured us: "No one takes it from me, but I lay it down on my own. . . ." (Jn 10:18).

When he was on trial he "opened not his mouth" in his own defense. Perhaps his silence was meant to help his accusers look within themselves and admit that they had no evidence against him. In this way, they could have been converted to his way of life.

Do we manage to remain silent when accused? Does our insecurity keep us on the defensive?

20 *But he was pierced for our offenses, / crushed for our sins, / Upon him was the chastisement that makes us whole, / by his stripes we were healed.* (Is 53:5)

The minute details of the dreadful passion and death of Jesus, foretold centuries before the Incarnation, prove to us how precisely and meticulously the Lord planned our salvation.

Our Savior was pierced and crushed because he assumed the chastisement for our sinfulness. Because he did this for us, we can now be healed and made whole. His impelling motive was his overwhelming love for each one of us: "No one has greater love than this, to lay down one's life for one's friends" (Jn 15:13).

He asks only our love in return.

HOLY SPIRIT

21 *. . . Thus says the LORD, who spreads out the heavens, lays the foundations of the earth, and forms the spirit of man within him.*

(Zec 12:1)

After the Father had created the world, and Jesus rescued the human race by his redemptive death, the Holy Spirit came to carry on the work of sanctification.

The Spirit strengthens our faith when we are assailed by fear and doubt and misgivings. He comforts us when we are weary or even brokenhearted. He brings us rest and relaxation as he fills us with his love, peace, and joy.

What more could the Lord do for us? Thank you, Father, Son, and Spirit!

22 *"Your good spirit you bestowed on them, to give them understanding; your manna you did not withold from their mouths, and you gave them water in their thirst."* (Neh 9:20)

Our Father is a most generous and provident God. Just as he provided the manna and water for his chosen people in the desert, so he continues to supply all our needs to sustain life and health.

But our Father knows that our needs aren't just physical, and he doesn't stop there. He bestows his Holy Spirit upon us to enrich us with the fullness of peace and joy, with an abundance of hope and a strong, fervent faith.

May our words and deeds bear witness to the provident care of our Father. May we demonstrate the love and power of the Holy Spirit to everyone we meet!

23 *Teach me to do your will, / for you are my God. / May your good spirit guide me / on level ground.* (Ps 143:10)

If we try to discern God's will in all our undertakings in life, we can be sure that our pathway will be level and smooth. The occasional hills and valleys are easily negotiated if we are walking in his will.

The "Good Spirit" will illumine our way and provide the strength and encouragement, the persistance and perseverance we need to continue our journey each day.

Lord, as we travel, fill us with the light of your radiant joy and take possession of our hearts.

24 *. . . I prayed, and prudence was given me; I pleaded, and the spirit of Wisdom came to me.* (Wis 7:7)

When we recognize our own poverty of spirit, acknowledge our utter dependence on the Lord, and pray for his help and guidance, we can be certain that the Holy Spirit will respond graciously and generously to our needs.

He will endow us with his gifts of wisdom and understanding to discern the will of the Lord. He will also give us the gifts of courage and fortitude enabling us to implement the will of the Lord in our daily encounters.

Holy Spirit, give us wisdom in our daily lives that we may do everything for the glory of God.

25 *"Lo! I will pour out to you my spirit, I will acquaint you with my words."* (Prv 1:23)

When Jesus said: "By their fruits you will know them" (Mt 7:16), he also meant that we can grow in our knowledge of the Holy Spirit by experiencing his powerful working in our midst.

Jesus promised that the Holy Spirit would enlighten us: "He will teach you everything and remind you of all that [I] told you" (Jn 14:26). Jesus promised furthermore that "When he comes, the Spirit of truth, he will guide you to all truth" (Jn 16:13).

Come, Holy Spirit, enlighten and guide us on our journey heavenward.

26 *"Could we find another like him ... a man so endowed with the spirit of God?"*

(Gn 41:38)

The Spirit of God manifested his divine wisdom through Joseph to such an extent that even Pharaoh gave witness to the power of God. Now the same Spirit who endowed Joseph with extraordinary wisdom abides with us. He will guide, instruct, and enlighten us about all our routine duties.

Come Holy Spirit, keep us open and receptive to your inspirations and discernment in all our daily undertakings!

27 *Until the spirit from on high / is poured out on us. / Then will the desert become an orchard / and the orchard be regarded as a forest.* (Is 32:15)

In pastoral imagery, the prophet attempts to describe to the pragmatic minds of his hearers the blessings of the Holy Spirit. Both the desert becoming an orchard and the orchard becoming a forest would seem to be tremendous blessings to them.

By the power of the Holy Spirit, we too, are being transformed as he cooperates with Jesus in reconciling us with the Father. In his own gentle way he leads us to goodness and holiness.

Come, Holy Spirit, clothe us with power to live the way of life to which we are called.

28 *For the holy spirit of discipline flees deceit and withdraws from senseless counsels; and when injustice occurs it is rebuked.* (Wis 1:5)

The Holy Spirit dwells within us as his temple, sanctifies us by leading us along the road to happiness and holiness. He enlightens us to what will bring us joy and peace. He gives us the power to avoid what would bring us distress and misery.

By his divine influence, the Holy Spirit can change hatred into love, sorrow into joy, anger into peace. He removes dissension and division. His love can change hearts.

O Holy Spirit, give us hearts that long for continual renewal!

29 *"I will give them a new heart and put a new spirit within them; . . . thus they shall be my people and I will be their God."* (Ez 11:19-20)

When we were baptized, we received a new spirit as we became the temples of the Holy Spirit, the source of divine love. His divine life and love within us transform our hearts to resemble more closely the heart of Jesus.

At the same time the Father adopted us as his children, making us his people, while he became our God in a richer, fuller way.

Let us praise and thank the Lord our God all the days of our life.

30 *Then afterward I will pour out my spirit upon all mankind. . . . in those days, I will pour out my spirit.* (Jl 3:1-2)

This prophecy was fulfilled in a special way on the day of Pentecost, as St. Peter acknowledged in his speech to the crowd who gathered that day.

The Holy Spirit continues to pour out his gifts and fruits upon every one of us all the days of our life. His abiding presence and love inspires and guides us, strengthens and encourages us, comforts and consoles us as we face the daily happenings in our lives.

O Holy Spirit, never abandon us!

HOLY TRINITY

31 *Here is my servant whom I uphold, / my chosen one with whom I am pleased, / Upon whom I have put my spirit; / he shall bring forth justice to the nations.* (Is 42:1)

In the Old Testament, we do not find any direct revelation of the doctrine of the Holy Trinity, but the work of all three Divine Persons is alluded to or mentioned many times.

In this text, the Father is presenting Jesus, his servant and chosen one, as the Redeemer of the world. He will be filled with the Holy

Spirit, who will remain to bring forth justice to the nations, thus implementing the fruits of the redemption.

In gratitude we say: Glory be to the Father, and to the Son, and to the Holy Spirit. Amen.

Encountering the Father, Son, and Holy Spirit in the Gospel

". . . Who do you say that I am?" (Mt 16:15)

FATHER

1 *"Look at the birds in the sky; they do not sow or reap, they gather nothing into barns, yet your heavenly Father feeds them. Are not you more important than they?"* (Mt 6:26)

God, our Father, loves us with a providential love. He provides for our every need each moment of the day. Jesus uses a powerful illustration to remind us of the deep, concerned love of the Father when he points to the birds in the sky who are cared for by their Creator.

Make a brief inventory of the blessings

showered upon you during the past hour, such as the oxygen you breathed, the sights you beheld, and sounds you heard. Such a recalling will increase your gratitude.

Father, let us sing your praises with the birds you feed so well!

2 *". . . Your heavenly Father knows that you need them all. But seek first the kingdom [of God] and his righteousness, and all these things will be given you besides."* (Mt 6:32-33)

Even though the Father knows all that we need, he wants us to ask him for those things we want. In doing so, we manifest our dependence upon him. Our interceding also keeps us aware that he is our gracious and provident Father.

As we continue to pray for a certain object, we must confront our need and place it openly before our Father. This can act to purify our petition. At times we may realize we are asking for something we really do not need. The exercise of presenting God with our needs can limit our frivolous desires.

Father, give us this day all that we truly need to serve you!

3 *"If you then, who are wicked, know how to give good gifts to your children, how much more will your heavenly Father give good things to those who ask him."* (Mt 7:11)

A devoted father loves his family and finds great joy and satisfaction in being able to provide a comfortable living for his wife and children. Due to human frailties, he may not be the perfect father, nor may he give them all he would like to give. They are grateful nonetheless.

Comparing the generosity of a human father with our heavenly Father, Jesus adds an infinite dimension, providential care, assuring us that the Father will fulfill all our needs on our journey through life.

In return the Father asks only a grateful heart.

4 *"... Whoever loves me will keep my word, and my Father will love him, and we will come to him and make our dwelling with him."*

(Jn 14:23)

When we love a person, we want to do everything to please that person. Furthermore, we want to be close to that person and share our life with our beloved.

When we love God, we want to please him by keeping his Word. We also long to be united with him and make him our constant companion.

Father, may your Word dwell in us in all its richness that we may thank and praise you all the days of our life in hymns, psalms, and spiritual canticles.

5 *"Be merciful, just as [also] your Father is merciful."* (Lk 6:36)

A merciful person is a kind, compassionate, and tolerant person. A merciful person has a mild disposition that readily overlooks the faults and failures of others.

Our loving Father in heaven is eminently and infinitely merciful. He manifests all the wonderful dispositions of a merciful God. When Jesus holds up the example of his Father, he challenges us to emulate this inexhaustible mercy and compassion.

Father, grant us the grace to become merciful and compassionate to everyone we meet today.

6 *At that time Jesus said in reply, "I give praise to you, Father, Lord of heaven and earth, for although you have hidden these things from the wise and the learned you have revealed them to the childlike."* (Mt 11:25)

No one is unimportant to our heavenly Father, regardless of age, education, or social standing. While the Father loves all his creatures with an unconditional love, he takes a special delight in the humble, simple souls who place all their faith and trust in him.

These persons are receptive to the power of his grace and receive his love graciously. They recognize their own poverty of spirit and acknowledge their dependence on the Lord, which pleases him very much. Jesus praised the Father for such people.

Father, help us to learn from Jesus who is meek and humble of heart.

7 *"My Father, who has given them [my sheep] to me, is greater than all, and no one can take them out of the Father's hand."* (Jn 10:29)

God, our Father, describes himself throughout the Old Testament as our Shepherd. The Father loves his sheep. He watches over us and provides for us. He protects us from anyone who would try to wean us away from him. This knowledge should remove any fear, worry, or anxiety from us and enable us to walk in peace and security.

However, Jesus cautions us that we must recognize the voice of the Shepherd and follow him whenever he calls.

Father, when you call us by name, give us a listening heart and a willing spirit.

8 *"I am the true vine, and my Father is the vine grower. He takes away every branch in me that does not bear fruit, and everyone that does he prunes so that it bears more fruit."* (Jn 15:1-2)

In this pastoral allegory, Jesus reminds us that the Father gently and carefully conditions us so that our life can become even more fruitful.

Trials and difficulties, pain and suffering in our lives are means which the Father uses to prune away whatever is restricting his grace from working within us. They are not punishments for something we have done wrong, but rather stepping stones leading us into a closer relationship with him.

Thank you, Father, for your loving care.

9 *If then you were raised with Christ, seek what is above, where Christ is seated at the right hand of God. Think of what is above, not of what is on earth.* (Col 3:1-2)

Throughout our earthly sojourn, we would do well to keep our focus on our loving Father and the kingdom which he has prepared for us. When we are able to do so, all the other concerns in life become more peripheral and less important.

This focus on our Father, and his care and concern for us, will dissolve many of the fears and worries which would otherwise plague us.

Gracious Father, thank you for your unbounded love for us as you await our coming to you.

10 *"... Holy Father, keep them in your name that you have given me, so that they may be one just as we are."* (Jn 17:11)

When we were baptized, we were initiated into the divine life of the Trinity, a community of perfect love. We are the family of God, the adopted sons and daughters of the Father. We are destined for that community of perfect love which lives in eternal union with the Lord.

With Jesus, we ask the Father to form us into a loving Christian community in this land of exile. This will prepare us for our total union with the Lord and all our brothers and sisters in heaven.

Yes, Father, we pray that we may be one as you are one in perfect love with Jesus and the Holy Spirit.

SON

11 *... "Where is the newborn king of the Jews? ..."* (Mt 2:2)

Based on the flimsy evidence of an unusual star and perhaps on some echoes of the prophecies made to the Jews, the Wise Men set out to pay tribute to "the newborn king of the Jews." They were dismayed that Herod knew nothing about the birth of the Messiah and could give them no directions to find him.

There are many worldly-wise persons today who are seeking the Lord without really knowing who or what they are seeking. They are only aware that there is a void in their lives which clamors to be filled.

Are we prepared to show them the way to Jesus? We do so not only by word, but also by our lifestyle. Lord Jesus, may all who we meet today go back "by another way" because your love and peace has radiated through us.

12 *It happened in those days that Jesus came from Nazareth of Galilee and was baptized in the Jordan by John.* (Mk 1:9)

In this brief statement, a whole way of life is changed for Jesus. We can well imagine the pain which accompanied this journey from Nazareth to the Jordan. Jesus had to leave his quiet, loving, peaceful, prayerful home to begin a public ministry which would end in rejection and death.

When the Lord calls us to a difficult or painful mission, we can reflect upon Jesus leaving home. We will find much comfort and strength in the realization that we are not traveling alone, but that he is with us.

"...I am with you always, until the end of the age" (Mt 28:20).

13 . . . *"Behold, the Lamb of God."* (Jn 1:36)

When John with his two disciples watched Jesus walk by, he pointed Jesus out with a brief, but significant statement. Every word was full of meaning. When John used the word "behold," he was asking his disciples to observe Jesus closely and listen intently if Jesus were to speak.

The lamb was not only the symbol of sacrifice, but the very victim to be offered. Enlightened by the Holy Spirit, John recognized Jesus as the Lamb of God who would be sacrificed to expiate the sins of mankind and to redeem the whole human race. John wanted his disciples to recognize Jesus as the promised Redeemer.

The prophetic words of Isaiah probably echoed in John's heart: "Like a lamb led to the slaughter" (Is 53:7).

Let us too behold the Lamb of God.

14 . . . *"I am the way and the truth and the life. No one comes to the Father except through me."* (Jn 14:6)

Jesus showed us the "way" by his teaching, especially as he invites us to live the Beatitudes, which he himself lived precisely.

Jesus is the "truth" because he proved the authenticity of his teaching by living every detail in his own life. He could honestly say: "I have given you a model. . . ."

Jesus is truly our "life" since he fills us with his own divine life, which will lead us eventually to the Father. Then we will receive it in all its fullness.

Jesus, keep us always close to you that we may come to the Father.

15 . . . *"I am the light of the world. Whoever follows me will not walk in darkness, but will have the light of life."* (Jn 8:12)

In Scripture, light is always symbolic of the presence of God. Jesus identifies himself as the light of the world leading us into eternal life.

By his gifts and grace, Jesus inspires us, enlightens us, and guides us along his way of life. He strengthens and encourages us when we falter or when the going becomes difficult.

Jesus, help us keep our focus always on you, our beacon light, as we journey through life.

16 *"I am the good shepherd. A good shepherd lays down his life for the sheep."* (Jn 10:11)

The scriptural image of the shepherd, which appears often in the Word of God, speaks volumes about caring, providing, nourishing, guiding, protecting, and above all, loving.

Jesus rightly identifies himself as the Good Shepherd. His whole life on earth reflects this role to an eminent degree. If there can be any doubt about his love, he gives us the clinching proof: "A good shepherd lays down his life for the sheep."

Jesus, teach us to respond to you, our Shepherd, with the confidence, trust, and docility of a gentle lamb.

17 *". . . Learn from me, for I am meek and humble of heart; and you will find rest for yourselves."* (Mt 11:29)

Jesus is the paragon of meekness and humility. Throughout his entire public ministry, he reflected a gentleness and humility of heart. His kind, docile disposition was evident in all his actions. He was never proud, arrogant, or vindictive.

He invites us, his followers, to become like him and radiate humility, meekness, and gentleness in our daily encounters with others. Such a disposition will greatly influence others and draw them to the Lord.

Jesus, meek and humble of heart, make our hearts like yours.

18 ... *"I am the bread of life; whoever comes to me will never hunger, and whoever believes in me will never thirst."* (Jn 6:35)

In scriptural language, bread is the gift which supplies all our needs. Jesus gave us himself in his Eucharistic Presence to strengthen our weak faith, to accompany and assist us in all the duties of each day, to encourage us in moments of trial and difficulty, and above all to prove his enduring love by abiding with us always.

When Jesus instituted the Eucharist at the Last Supper, his request was quite imperative: "Do this in memory of me" (Lk 22:19).

Jesus, help us to fathom more deeply the mystery of such a boundless love.

19 ... *"This is my chosen Son; listen to him."* (Lk 9:35)

On Mount Tabor at the Transfiguration, the voice of the Father identified Jesus as his "chosen Son," and also urged us to listen to him. Jesus was about to begin his journey to Jerusalem to face his passion and death. The faith of many would be weakened as Jesus seemed to go down in defeat. The voice of the Father endorsed this mission as part of the divine plan for our redemption and salvation.

The Father's admonition, "listen to him," was intended to help us to understand the mystery of suffering in our own lives.

Father, in moments of pain and distress, help us to say with your Son, "not my will but yours be done" (Lk 22:42).

20 *As he drew near, he saw the city and wept over it, saying, "If this day you only knew what makes for peace—but now it is hidden from your eyes."* (Lk 19:41-42)

Jesus experienced all the human emotions which we feel, but to a much greater degree since his human nature was not scarred by any sinfulness. He had come to redeem and save his people, but they turned a deaf ear to his pleading. His heart was so overwhelmed by their rejection that he wept bitter tears.

Today Jesus receives the same rejection. He must weep over those who turn away from him or refuse to accept him. Do we pray for them?

Do we ever give Jesus any cause to weep over us?

HOLY SPIRIT

21 ... *"The holy Spirit will come upon you, and the power of the Most High will overshadow you. Therefore the child to be born will be called holy, the Son of God."* (Lk 1:35)

The immediate preparation for the coming of the long-promised Redeemer of the human race began with the mystery of the Incarnation. As the angel indicated, this redemption is the work of the Holy Trinity.

The Father sent the Holy Spirit to overshadow Mary as she conceived Jesus the Messiah. After Jesus made the supreme act of love and laid down his life for us, he sent the Holy Spirit to dwell within us and guide us to our eternal destiny.

All this was possible because of Mary's unqualified fiat to the Lord. Mother Mary, help us to say "Yes" to the Lord regardless of what he may ask.

22 *"For at the moment the sound of your greeting reached my ears, the infant in my womb leaped for joy."* (Lk 1:44)

Enlightened by the Holy Spirit, Elizabeth recognized Mary as the mother of the Messiah. The powerful influence of the Holy Spirit went even beyond these two expectant mothers. The unborn John leaped with joy at the presence of Jesus still hidden in his mother's womb. This recognition is a manifestation of the powerful influence of the Holy Spirit not only in the life of John, but in our lives as well.

John, pray that we may always respond to the inspirations of the Holy Spirit and permit him to transform us according to his divine plan that we also may leap with joy.

23 *". . . He will be filled with the holy Spirit even from his mother's womb, and he will turn many of the children of Israel to the Lord their God."* (Lk 1:15-16)

When God calls anyone to a specific mission, he endows him or her with all the gifts and graces necessary to accomplish the undertaking. His principal gift is the gift of the Holy Spirit who inspires, enlightens, guides, and strengthens the person to fulfill the task.

However, the person must be open and receptive to the influence of the Holy Spirit. John the Baptist gave us an ideal example of being receptive to and cooperative with the gifts of the Holy Spirit. The angel foretold that John would be a powerful preacher and a great precursor only because he was anointed by the Holy Spirit.

Ask his intercession that we may be open and receptive at all times.

24 *John testified further, saying, "I saw the Spirit come down like a dove from the sky and remain upon him."* (Jn 1:32)

At the baptism of Jesus, the Holy Spirit appeared in the form of a dove, which is the symbol of peace. Jesus came to preach the way to that peace which the world cannot give. He sacrificed his life to gain eternal peace, *shalom,* which is salvation.

The dove is also an appropriate and popular symbol of the Holy Spirit, the very source of peace. Peace is one of the special fruits of the Spirit. He guides and directs us to genuine peace by his inspirations, enlightenment, and support on our pilgrim way.

Come, Holy Spirit, pour out your love, peace, and joy upon us.

25 *Filled with the holy Spirit, Jesus returned from the Jordan and was led by the Spirit into the desert for forty days, to be tempted by the devil. . . .* (Lk 4:1)

The Holy Spirit teaches us a valuable lesson in leading Jesus into the desert to be tempted by the devil. Temptations help us to grow and mature spiritually. They enable us to recognize our own weakness and teach us to depend more and more on the Lord.

The Holy Spirit helps us to discern the

subtleties of the evil one before the temptation becomes overpowering.

When temptations arise we can use a brief, but powerful exorcism: "In the name of Jesus, I drive you out."

26 *"The Spirit of the Lord is upon me, / because he has anointed me / to bring glad tidings to the poor. . . ."* (Lk 4:18)

Jesus himself was guided by the Holy Spirit in his ministry. His docility to the influence of the Holy Spirit is a model and example for us.

Jesus testified that the Holy Spirit is dynamic and operative in the work of our salvation. He made of us his temple in order to live with us and accompany us so he can be our daily companion.

O Holy Spirit, we stand in need of your guidance and grace at all times. Give us a quiet listening heart and a responsive spirit.

27 *"I have baptized you with water; he will baptize you with the holy Spirit."* (Mk 1:8)

Jesus gave us the Sacrament of Baptism, in which we become temples of the Holy Spirit and special members of the family of God. The Holy Spirit's abiding presence and power enable us to meet the challenges of each day.

The Father also comes to us in baptism. He assures us: "I will live with them and move among them, / and I will be their God / and they shall be my people" (2 Cor 6:16).

Thank you, O Holy Spirit, for the honor, privilege, and dignity you have bestowed on us in our baptism. We count on your power, enlightenment, strength, and love to help us all the days of our lives.

28 *". . . I will ask the Father, and he will give you another Advocate to be with you always, the Spirit of truth, which the world cannot accept, because it neither sees nor knows it. . . ."*
(Jn 14:16-17)

Jesus promised that he would not leave us orphans, but that he would come back to us and remain with us always. He has fulfilled this promise, since the presence of the Holy Spirit within us is the fullness of Jesus abiding with us. Our faith assures us of his powerful presence.

The Father, too, stays with us for he said, "I will be a father to you, / and you shall be sons and daughters to me" (2 Cor 6:18).

Holy Spirit, continue to strengthen our faith. May it radiate to others who are less inclined to believe.

29 *"The Advocate, the holy Spirit that the Father will send in my name—he will teach you everything and remind you of all that [I] told you."* (Jn 14:26)

The Holy Spirit dwells within us to teach us how to translate the Gospel message into our day-to-day living, to meet the secular culture surrounding us. If we act out of conviction, we may have to suffer some subtle persecution or be labeled out of step with the times.

We need divine inspiration in an age which is so materialistically oriented. We need the strength and encouragement of the Holy Spirit to dare to be different in a world which is so indifferent to the Lord.

"Come, Holy Spirit, fill the hearts of your faithful and enkindle in them the fire of your love."

30 *"I have much more to tell you, but you cannot bear it now. But when he comes, the Spirit of truth, he will guide you to all truth. . . ."* (Jn 16:12-13)

One of the special gifts the Holy Spirit bestows on us is the gift of discernment of spirits. Discernment helps us determine whether our thoughts, desires, and inclinations come from God, are ruses from the evil one, or reflect our own selfish ambitions.

In trying to lead us away from the Lord, the devil is extremely subtle. He presents evil as something good, useful, and even necessary for us, then turns it for his own ends.

O Spirit of God, help me discern what is truly divine inspiration, and also give me the will to follow it.

HOLY TRINITY

31 *After Jesus was baptized, he came up from the water and behold, the heavens were opened [for him], and he saw the Spirit of God descending like a dove [and] coming upon him. And a voice came from the heavens, saying, "This is my beloved Son, with whom I am well pleased."*
(Mt 3:16-17)

This theophany (manifestation) of the Trinity clarifies the specific role of each Divine Person. The Father sent his Son as our Redeemer. ". . . God so loved the world that he gave his only Son . . ." (Jn 3:16).

Jesus showed the need of repentance by himself submitting to the penitential rite of baptism, while the Holy Spirit appeared as a dove to anoint Jesus as he began his ministry. The Father also confirmed the role of Jesus as teacher: "This is my beloved Son, with whom I am well pleased."

This same Godhead is dwelling within us to enable us to reach the glory of our permanent home in heaven.

Listening to the Father, Son, and Holy Spirit in the Epistles

"In the foreknowledge of God the Father, through sanctification by the Spirit, for obedience and sprinkling with the blood of Jesus Christ: may grace and peace be yours in abundance." (1 Pt 1:2)

FATHER

1 *... For us there is / one God, the Father, / from whom all things are and for whom we exist ...*
(1 Cor 8:6)

God must always be center stage in our lives. Our focus must always be directed toward him and our hearts attuned to his plans for us. St. Paul advises us: "Think of

57

what is above, not of what is on earth'' (Col 3:2).

God has created everything which exists. As we use and enjoy his countless gifts, we are pleasing our gracious Father and progressing steadily on our way to eternal union with him.

Father, you are a God of might and power, but you are a gentle loving Father to us. Thank you, Father.

2 *... We are the temple of the living God; as God said: / "I will live with them and move among them, / and I will be their God / and they shall be my people."* (2 Cor 6:16)

The transcendent God of heaven and earth, the Creator and Sustainer of the entire universe, claims us as his very own people. We are the "temple of the living God."

He is not only our God, but also our loving Father nurturing and caring for us with every breath we take. What a singular privilege is ours! What greater dignity could we have!

Abba, Father.

3 *See what love the Father has bestowed on us that we may be called the children of God. Yet so we are. . . .* (1 Jn 3:1)

A person who loves another person wants to be closely associated with that person. He or she wants to share his or her life with the beloved. If this is true of human love, with all its limitations, how much truer is it of God's unbounded love for us?

The Father adopted us as his children in order to share his greatest gift with us, the gift of himself in the divine life and love which he imparts to us. This gift is but a prelude to the total immersion in his divine life which awaits us in heaven.

Thank you, Father, for loving us. We love you, too.

4 *All good giving and every perfect gift is from above, coming down from the Father of lights, with whom there is no alteration or shadow caused by change.* (Jas 1:17)

The Father loves us with an infinite love which expresses itself in providing for all our needs. As the Father of lights, he rules over the sun, moon, and stars. Although these lights give us consistency in time and seasons, they also change from their lowest point to their zenith.

Unlike the lights, the Father's love is immutable and consistent. There is never any change or alteration. Only we change as we open wide to receive his love, or as we limit it by fearing to be totally receptive since the Lord may ask too much.

Thank you, Father, for all your gifts, especially your lights—sun, moon, and stars.

5 *One God and Father of all, who is over all and through all and in all.* (Eph 4:6)

In the first commandment the Father says: "I, the LORD, am your God. . . . You shall not have other gods besides me" (Dt 5:6-7). We profess that same truth each time we pray in the Creed: "We believe in one God, the Father, the Almighty, maker of heaven and earth and all that is seen and unseen."

This conviction means that God should occupy the number-one priority in our lives. We need to be on our guard lest false gods, such as business, secular pursuits, or worldly demands take precedence. An occasional survey of life would be profitable.

Father, we want you to be "over all and through all and in all" that we do.

6 *"... I will be a father to you, / and you shall be sons and daughters to me, / says the Lord Almighty."* (2 Cor 6:18)

We are proud of our heritage and the human family the Lord gave us. We are grateful to our human fathers for their dedication and love for us. We strive to show our appreciation by making them proud of us.

Our heavenly Father is also proud of us. He is pleased when we strive to become the person he wants us to be by following his Fatherly directives.

Thank you, Lord, for being a Father to us.

7 *As proof that you are children, God sent the spirit of his Son into our hearts, crying out, "Abba, Father!"* (Gal 4:6)

The startling mystery that God is our loving Father whom we may call "Abba" is too profound for us to grasp. A sense of unworthiness immediately limits our comprehension of this truth. Our Abba sent his Spirit to help us understand how much he loves us and wants us for his adopted sons and daughters.

The awareness of this unique privilege also challenges us to live our lives according to his will by reflecting his love, peace, and joy all around us.

Abba, Father, may we never disappoint you.

8 *That the God of our Lord Jesus Christ, the Father of glory, may give you a spirit of wisdom and revelation resulting in knowledge of him.* (Eph 1:17)

While Jesus was on earth he revealed many things about the Father. Much of this information contributed to our intellectual knowledge of God. However, we must not only know about a person with our mind, but also with our heart to truly love him or her.

This desired heart knowledge of God is the fruit of our prayer. The prayer of listening, sometimes called prayer of the heart, gives us insights into the person of God which our reason could never attain. This is the wisdom and revelation for which we pray.

9 *What agreement has the temple of God with idols? For we are the temple of the living God . . .* (2 Cor 6:16)

When Jesus called us to follow him, the Father adopted us as his children. We became the temple of the living God. Our response to his call set us apart from the world of idols. We now dare to be different because we belong to God.

Jesus prepared us for the fact that we may not be accepted by the world at all times. "... You do not belong to the world, and I have chosen you out of the world, the world hates you" (Jn 15:19). However, we are in good company for Jesus also said: ". . . If they persecuted me, they will also persecute you. . . ." (Jn 15:20).

10 *To our God and Father, glory for ever and ever. Amen.* (Phil 4:20)

We give glory to God our Father by offering him worshipful praise, honor, and thanksgiving for his infinite goodness and magnificence. Our prime duty in life is to glorify the transcendent God of heaven and earth who is, at the same time, our caring, concerned Father.

When our hearts are filled with awe and wonder toward such a benevolent Father, praise and thanksgiving automatically rise to our thoughts and words.

May we glorify our bountiful Father all the days of our life.

SON

11 *Whoever acknowledges that Jesus is the Son of God, God remains in him and he in God.* (1 Jn 4:15)

To acknowledge that Jesus is the Son of God requires faith on our part. When reason fails to grasp a mystery, faith takes over. Our earnest profession and consistent practice of faith will ensure the Lord remaining with us.

We are Christians because of the indwelling of the Lord. Our lifestyle gives witness to his abiding presence, radiating through us.

If we were accused of being a Christian, would there be enough evidence to convict us?

12 *It is due to him that you are in Christ Jesus, who became for us wisdom from God, as well as righteousness, sanctification, and redemption.* (1 Cor 1:30)

Jesus came into the world to be our Savior. He redeemed our fallen human nature and enabled us to share in God's divine life and love. He is sanctifying us by pouring out upon us his Holy Spirit, the Sanctifier. The Spirit helps us avoid sin and grow in our spiritual life.

Jesus is "righteousness" personified, as he himself said: "Can any of you charge me with sin?'' (Jn 8:46). Now he challenges us to live his way of life as he helps us avoid sin and grow in our love for God and neighbor.

He "became for us wisdom from God" by giving us the desire and determination to walk his pathway through life.

13 *"For the Lamb who is in the center of the throne will shepherd them / and lead them to springs of life-giving water, / and God will wipe away every tear from their eyes." (Rv 7:17)*

Not even under the inspiration of the Holy Spirit could the scriptural author find words to define adequately God's out-pouring of his love in heaven. The "springs of life-giving water" image is a feeble at-tempt to describe the boundless, enduring love of God which will overwhelm us in our eternal home.

This is the unimaginable love which is awaiting us when the Lord calls us to himself.

14 *. . . As you received Christ Jesus the Lord, walk in him, rooted in him and built upon him and established in the faith as you were taught, abounding in thanksgiving. (Col 2:6-7)*

These inspired words of encouragement from St. Paul are meant especially for us. Since Jesus came to live with us, we are to "walk with him," keeping ourselves aware that we are not alone, but he is walking with us. He will be the first concern of our lives if we are aware of his continuous presence with us.

If we are "rooted in him and built upon him," his grace will influence our decisions and his strength will empower our every action.

As we strive to function with the awareness of his loving presence, we will abound in thanksgiving.

15 *This saying is trustworthy and deserves full acceptance: Christ Jesus came into the world to save sinners. . . .* (1 Tm 1:15)

Jesus came to restore our fragmented relationship with the Father. He himself said: "I have not come to call the righteous to repentance, but sinners" (Lk 5:32). Jesus proved his intention as he identified with sinners and reached out to them with his forgiving, healing, redeeming love.

Today the glory of Jesus is to continue his redemptive work among us. He is always eager and anxious to forgive us when we come to him with humble, contrite hearts.

Thank you, Lord Jesus, for your forgiving, healing, redeeming love.

16 *"I, Jesus, sent my angel to give you this testimony for the churches. I am the root and offspring of David, the bright morning star."*
(Rv 22:16)

Jesus calls himself the "morning star" because he is a bright light guiding us through the maze of sin, error, hatred, violence, and confusion that surrounds us. If we follow Jesus' way of life, he will free us from this maze and lead us safely and securely to our eternal destiny.

St. Peter writes: "You will do well to be attentive to it, as to a lamp shining in a dark place, until day dawns and the morning star rises in your hearts" (2 Pt 1:19).

Thank you, Lord, for being the light of the world.

17 *... Like living stones, let yourselves be built into a spiritual house to be a holy priesthood to offer spiritual sacrifices acceptable to God through Jesus Christ.* (1 Pt 2:5)

Our purpose in life is to give ourselves with all that we do to the Lord. In the Eucharistic celebration, Jesus devised a privileged means by which we could make the oblation of self by uniting it to the gift of himself to the Father. Even though our giving of self may be half-hearted or distracted at times, Jesus purifies and sanctifies it by adding the infinite dimension of his own love.

We are a privileged people and a holy priesthood. Our spiritual offerings will bring untold blessings to ourselves and to our world.

May we be a tiny stone in the "spiritual house."

18 *... We also boast of God through our Lord Jesus Christ, through whom we have now received reconciliation.* (Rom 5:11)

Sin severed man's relationship with God by depriving sinners of their share of his divine life. By his supreme act of reconciliation, Jesus restored our friendship with the Father by recreating in us the potential to share in this life.

How delighted our compassionate Father is to have us in communion with him once again. How pleased he is with Jesus, who reconciled us with him. Listen to the Father as he says: "This is my beloved Son, with whom I am well pleased; listen to him" (Mt 17:5).

Lord Jesus, our Redeemer, keep our bond increasingly strong.

19 *Have among yourselves the same attitude that is also yours in Christ Jesus.*

(Phil 2:5)

As we spend time listening with our own heart to the heart of Jesus, our attitudes will gradually become similar to his attitudes. We become what we contemplate. As we contemplate the heart of Jesus, we will become like him.

Behold his heart: so patient with the disciples; reaching out in empathy to the widow of Naim; moved with pity for the sick and suffering, the poor and the downtrodden; weeping for his own people who rejected him; and yet still filled with mercy and forgiveness for all sinners, with love for all people.

His heart is yearning for our love in return!

20 *. . . If we walk in the light as he is in the light, then we have fellowship with one another, and the blood of his Son Jesus cleanses us from all sin.* (1 Jn 1:7)

In Scripture, light means the presence of God while darkness stands for evil. If we walk in the presence of God, we are in the light, since Jesus cleanses us from all sin.

Our interior disposition is the first essential for receiving his merciful forgiveness. We need to recognize sin for what it really is—a refusal to love. We must acknowledge our sinfulness humbly and sincerely as we seek his pardon and forgiveness.

Jesus, help us to walk always in your light and experience the peace and joy which only you can give.

HOLY SPIRIT

21 *The Spirit itself bears witness with our spirit that we are children of God.*

(Rom 8:16)

When we receive the Holy Spirit, he does not come to us empty-handed. He fills us with his many gifts to enable us to live according to God's divine plan.

The Spirit gives us the gift of knowledge and understanding to help us comprehend the great dignity which is ours as the adopted children of God. He helps us respond in love and humility as we receive the many privileges accorded us in the family of God. He endows us with the gift of wisdom to see more distinctly the pathway the Lord wants us to follow.

Spirit of God, enlighten our spirit to say yes to the will of the Lord at all times.

22 *For the kingdom of God is not a matter of food and drink, but of righteousness, peace, and joy in the holy Spirit.* (Rom 14:17)

The ancient Hebrews believed that if a person lived a good life, God would reward him or her with the material gifts of health and wealth. In our Christian dispensation, we know that one of the gifts of the Holy Spirit is to lead us to holiness of life which brings with it great peace and joy which the world cannot give.

The kingdom of God does not consist for us of the gifts "of food and drink." The kingdom of God means that the Lord himself dwells with us here and now and in all his fullness in the world to come.

Holy Spirit, may our journey to our eternal kingdom be peaceful and joyous.

23 *We have not received the spirit of the world but the Spirit that is from God, so that we may understand the things freely given us by God.* (1 Cor 2:12)

We admire a person who is knowledgeable about many things. God is also pleased when we use our intellect to acquire knowledge which will increase our ability to work more professionally and productively.

However, try as we might, we cannot fathom the mysterious workings of the Lord with our human knowledge alone. We need the special inspiration and enlightenment of the Holy Spirit. Since he is the Spirit of wisdom and understanding, he freely shares these gifts with us. He also gives us the fortitude to put them into practice.

Holy Spirit, grant us the grace to use your gifts gratefully and humbly.

24 *Now the Spirit explicitly says that in the last times some will turn away from the faith by paying attention to deceitful spirits and demonic instructions.* (1 Tm 4:1)

These inspired words may well apply to our own times. There is a great crisis in faith rampant in our world today. The tremendous progress we have made in technology has made us a very proud and sophisticated people who seem to have little need of God. As our faith in God weakens, we lose confidence and trust in others. Our society's sense of sin is waning, and some are apt to deny its existence. Cults of various types are increasing in popularity.

Today's crisis in faith means that each of us is being called to live a life governed by a vibrant, dynamic faith in God and in others.

25 *. . . Do not grieve the holy Spirit of God, with which you were sealed for the day of redemption.* (Eph 4:30)

Jesus uses some frightening language in speaking of the sins against the Holy Spirit: "Whoever blasphemes against the holy Spirit will never have forgiveness, but is guilty of an everlasting sin" (Mk 3:29). The malice of these sins consists of a refusal to acknowledge or accept forgiveness by attributing the work of the Holy Spirit to the devil.

We can also grieve the Holy Spirit by less
malicious sins, such as refusing to accept
and cooperate with his graces or neglecting
to use the many gifts he has given us. These
can be forgiven.

O Holy Spirit, may we never grieve you!

26 *. . . The Spirit too comes to the aid of our
weakness; for we do not know how to pray
as we ought, but the Spirit itself intercedes with
inexpressible groanings.* (Rom 8:26)

The very desire to pray and the motivation we need are all gifts of the Holy Spirit.
He envelops our spirit as he draws us into
an experience of the divine. He enlightens
our minds to understand God's plan and
strengthens us to accomplish it in our lives.

The experience of his presence, the feeling
of being loved and the peace and joy which
fill our hearts are all gifts of the Holy Spirit.

"Lord, teach us to pray" (Lk 11:1).

27 *. . . No prophecy ever came through human
will; but rather human beings moved by the
holy Spirit spoke under the influence of God.*
(2 Pt 1:21)

God inspired the prophets of old to reveal
his will to his people. These prophets reminded the people again and again how
precisely they were to respond to the Lord's
commands. They themselves put into prac-

tice the way of life they had taught.

The Lord raises up certain prophets in every age to teach and instruct, to enlighten and guide us in the way of the Lord. These persons are especially endowed by the Holy Spirit to fulfill this important ministry. No one can assume this office, but must be chosen by the Holy Spirit. St. John tells us to test every spirit. The best test for someone who claims to represent the Lord is the witness of his or her own life.

Lord, give us listening hearts.

28 *If you are insulted for the name of Christ, blessed are you, for the Spirit of glory and of God rests upon you.* (1 Pt 4:14)

As we strive to live the Christian way of life proclaimed and demonstrated by Jesus, we can be certain that we will be criticized, perhaps even persecuted. One simple reason for the upraised eyebrows or smirky smile, the subtle or open persecution is that our way of life is a silent and unintended attack on the critic's worldly way of life.

It takes courage to dare to be different from the world and to stand firmly on our own principles. Jesus prepared us for this reaction to our Christlike living. To encourage us lest we lose heart, Jesus pronounced a special Beatitude:

"Blessed are they who are persecuted for
the sake of righteousness,
for theirs is the kingdom of heaven."
(Mt 5:10)

29 *Those who keep his commandments remain in him, and he in them, and the way we know that he remains in us is from the Spirit that he gave us.* (1 Jn 3:24)

Jesus promised us that if we love him and keep his word, both he and the Father will come and make their dwelling with us (Jn 14:23). This astounding truth is hard for us to fathom, that the eternal, almighty, transcendent God of heaven and earth would deign to make us his special dwelling place.

We can accept this wonderful truth only because the Spirit has endowed us with the gift of faith. Jesus assures us that we will be able to know and live this truth only because the Spirit "remains with you, and will be in you" (Jn 14:17).

30 *If the Spirit of the one who raised Jesus from the dead dwells in you, the one who raised Christ from the dead will give life to your mortal bodies also, through his Spirit that dwells in you.* (Rom 8:11)

The whole body of our Catholic beliefs is authenticated by the great truth of the resurrection of Jesus from the dead. By his death Jesus redeemed our human nature, and by his rising from the dead, he shared with us his divine life.

We enter into the process of our own resurrection at the time of our baptism when the Holy Spirit establishes his temple within us. Since we are still in our "mortal bodies," we share in his divine life in a limited way. When we finally shed our mortal coil, we shall rise with Jesus to enjoy the fullness of his divine life.

This will be our resurrection! Alleluia. Alleluia.

HOLY TRINITY

31 *... Be filled with the Spirit. . . . giving thanks always and for everything in the name of our Lord Jesus Christ to God the Father.*
(Eph 5:18, 20)

The Holy Spirit, dynamic within us, helps us recognize, acknowledge, and appreciate all the gifts we receive each day. Our own thanks seem so inadequate until we offer them in union with Jesus to the Father.

Each time we celebrate Mass, a powerful prayer of thanksgiving, we offer the Father our grateful hearts. We give him the gift of ourselves along with Jesus our eternal high priest.

All glory and honor to you Father, Son, and Holy Spirit. Amen.

God's Love Creates

Above all, give praise to your Creator, / who showers his favors upon you. (Sir 32:13)

FATHER

1 *God created man in his image; / in the divine image he created him; / male and female he created them.* (Gn 1:27)

Every individual person is a masterpiece of God's creation. Our human body is one of the most intricate machines which could ever be made. In an even more important miracle than this physical one, we are created in the divine image.

Our humanity is dignified by the indwelling of the Lord. Little wonder that the psalmist exclaimed:

What is man that you should be mindful of him, / or the son of man that you should care for him? (Ps 8:5)

2 *God looked at everything he had made, and he found it very good.* (Gn 1:31)

God created the world and everything in it for our sustenance and enjoyment. Creation is a dynamic expression of love in action. The universe is only a partial revelation of God's mighty power and a faint reflection of his exquisite beauty. That beauty awaits us in heaven.

As we pause and prayerfully ponder our Father's creating love, we, too, will find it "very good." As we listen we will detect his voice saying "I did this all for you, because I love you."

3 *. . . The creator of the heavens, / who is God, / The designer and maker of the earth who established it, / Not creating it to be a waste, / but designing it to be lived in: / I am the LORD, and there is no other.* (Is 45:18)

The beauty of a tree-lined lane, the roar of a waterfall cascading down a mountainside, the richness of fertile field yielding a plentiful harvest—all are visible evidence that God did not create our earth "to be a waste."

Unfortunately, either motivated by greed or by sheer neglect and carelessness, we have done so much to mar the beauty of God as reflected in his creation.

We thank and praise you Lord, for your patience with us.

4 *The clear vault of the sky shines forth / like heaven itself, a vision of glory. / The orb of the sun, resplendent at its rising: / what a wonderful work of the Most High!* (Sir 43:1-2)

When we witness the splendor of a brilliant morning sunrise, or behold the magnificence of an evening sunset, our hearts naturally exalt in joy and praise of our Almighty Father, who reflects only a minute detail of his beauty in creation.

Father, we thank you for the wonderful work of your creation for our sustenance and enjoyment. Help us to pause frequently to thank and praise you for your goodness to us.

5 *Truly you have formed my inmost being; you knit me in my mother's womb. / I give you thanks that I am fearfully, wonderfully made: / wonderful are your works. . . .*
(Ps 139:13-14)

Every conception and birth is a manifestation of God's creative love. God empowers parents to share in his creative power.

We were conceived and born because God planned it from all eternity. He loved us so much that he wanted us to live and experience his unfathomable love.

Yes, Lord, "I give you thanks that I am fearfully, wonderfully made."

6 *"I do not know how you came into existence in my womb; it was not I who gave you the breath of life, nor was it I who set in order the elements of which each of you is composed. Therefore, since it is the Creator of the universe who shapes each man's beginning, as he brings about the origin of everything, he, in his mercy, will give you back both breath and life, because you now disregard yourselves for the sake of his law."*

(2 Mc 7:22-23)

The mystery of motherhood is so sacred and so profound that not even mothers can comprehend it, even though they are so personally overshadowed with the Lord's creative love.

This mother in the Book of Maccabees experienced God's creative love so deeply that she was able to respond by offering the Lord her seven sons and herself.

Lord, embrace all mothers, especially our own, enveloping them in the warmth and glow of your divine love.

7 *The LORD's are the earth and its fullness; / the world and those who dwell in it. / For he founded it upon the seas / and established it upon the rivers.* (Ps 24:1-2)

God's infinite love found expression in creating everything seen and unseen, every person known or unknown to us. The fullness of the earth is a faint reflection of his beauty. The bountifulness of the earth is the gift of his caring, concerned love.

Today, pause to breathe in his gift of oxygen, to smell and admire a flower, to listen to the sounds of silence, to enjoy the love of a beloved.

These are ways of saying "thank you" to the Lord and praising him for his goodness.

8 *The heavens declare the glory of God, / and the firmament proclaims his handiwork.*
(Ps 19:2)

On a clear night the heavenly galaxies, the silvery moon, the myriad twinkling stars all bespeak the glory of God.

Throughout the day the azure blue vault of heaven with its fleecy and cumulus clouds raises our hearts and minds to glorify the exquisite beauty of the creative love of so good a Father.

Father, help us to take the time to behold, absorb, admire, and enjoy the magnificent beauty you have created for us.

9 *. . . The LORD is the eternal God, / creator of the ends of the earth . . .* (Is 40:28)

The ends of the earth, with all their hidden secrets, are the handiwork of our eternal God. The recent monumental discoveries in technology are unraveling some of the mysteries of his creative genius.

Each new discovery should draw us into a deeper appreciation of the immensity of his unfathomable love which fashioned everything from the mightiest mountain to the tiniest atom to serve our needs.

"Let all your works give you thanks, O LORD . . ." (Ps 145:10).

10

"Worthy are you, Lord our God, / to receive glory and honor and power, / for you created all things; / because of your will they came to be and were created." (Rv 4:11)

As we enjoy the ever-changing hues of an evening's sunset, or admire the immensity of a massive mountain, or marvel at the speed and mobility of a tiny insect, or the dexterity of our own hand, we are praising and glorifying the Lord, our God, as the Creator of all things.

Thank you, loving Father, for giving us the ability to enjoy the beauty of all your creation. Help me to behold your creating love reflected in everything we see, hear, smell, touch, and taste this day.

SON

11 *All things came to be through him, / and without him nothing came to be. / What came to be through him was life, / and this life was the light of the human race.* (Jn 1:3-4)

In the Gospel, John introduces Jesus as the Creator of all that came to be. John wanted to underscore the inexhaustible love of Jesus expressed in the countless works of creation.

Jesus came to create an invisible gift which is even greater and more magnificent. He redeemed us so that "through him was life."

The splendor of his visible creation is only a glimpse into the beauty that we will enjoy when he shares this divine life with us more fully in heaven.

12 *He was in the world, / and the world came to be through him, / but the world did not know him.* (Jn 1:10)

Given our scarred human nature, we take so many gifts for granted. We accept countless blessings every day with little or no thought of the gracious Creator who provided them. Even though "the world came to be through him [Jesus]," the world does not know him nor even thank him.

Create a new heart in us, Lord, a heart fully aware and grateful for the manifold gifts of your creation, a heart filled with praise and thanksgiving.

We thank you, too, Lord, for someone who does not, nor ever has, thanked you.

13 *And the Word became flesh / and made his dwelling among us, / and we saw his glory, / the glory as of the Father's only Son, / full of grace and truth.* (Jn 1:14)

The Incarnation of Jesus, and especially his coming as a helpless, vulnerable child, will always remain a unique mystery. The "how" of the Incarnation is not as important as the "why" of the God of heaven and earth becoming one of us.

Jesus took on our human nature so that he could take it down to death with himself and redeem us. All this was prompted by his infinite love for us personally and individually. "No one has greater love than this, to lay down one's life for one's friends" (Jn 15:13).

The only return the Lord asks is our loving service in fulfilling his will which will bring us eternal union with him.

14 *In these last days, he spoke to us through a son, whom he made heir of all things and through whom he created the universe, / who is the refulgence of his glory, / the very imprint of his being, . . .* (Heb 1:2-3)

Long before Jesus came into the world to redeem us, he had created the universe as "the refulgence of his glory, the very imprint of his being."

Our aim in life is to recognize his caring, concerned love shown in every facet of creation. As we contemplate the imprint of his transcendence all around us, we stand in awe and wonder.

May our hearts swell with praise and thanksgiving throughout the moments of the day.

15 *"Then the king will say to those on his right, 'Come, you who are blessed by my Father. Inherit the kingdom prepared for you from the foundation of the world.'"* (Mt 25:34)

The kingdom was prepared for us since the foundation of the world, but sin barred our entry into the glory of the kingdom. By his redemptive death and resurrection, Jesus created a glorified life which he shares with us. This qualifies us to enter into the joy and happiness of that kingdom.

We pave our way into the kingdom by helping to fulfill, with love, the needs we encounter each day. Jesus pointed out a few of those common needs: feeding the hungry, giving drink to the thirsty, etc.

". . . Whatever you did for one of these least brothers of mine, you did for me" (Mt 25:40).

16 *". . . Whoever drinks the water I shall give will never thirst; the water I shall give will become in him a spring of water welling up to eternal life."* (Jn 4:14)

When Jesus speaks of water, he means "living water" which is his divine life. He alone can satisfy all our longings and desires. Only in him can we find fulfillment, since he is the source of love, peace, and joy through the workings of the Holy Spirit.

Jesus wants to share these gifts with us, for they are the fruits of his divine life. As we permit his divine life and love to increase and mature in us, we are progressing well along the road to eternal life.

Lord, we praise and thank you for your infinite goodness.

17 *Jesus answered and said to her, "If you knew the gift of God and who is saying to you, 'Give me a drink,' you would have asked him and he would have given you living water."*

(Jn 4:10)

Jesus always accommodated himself to our human limitations. He knew that the Samaritan woman could not grasp the concept of divine life which he was eager to share with her. He used terminology which she could comprehend—"living water."

This expression speaks eloquently to us also, since water is so essential to our physical well-being. Likewise, his divine love—"living water"— is absolutely essential for our life here and hereafter.

Thank you, Lord, for precious water and eternal thanks for "living water."

18 *Stop lying to one another, since you have taken off the old self with its practices and have put on the new self, which is being renewed, for knowledge, in the image of its creator.*

(Col 3:9-10)

In the inspired account of creation we read: "God created man in his image; / in the divine image he created him" (Gn 1:27). Our physical image is not a replica of God, even though our bodies are the most intricate and perfect machine ever made. Rather, we become like God by putting on the "new self''—Christlikeness—by having the mind and heart of Jesus within us. We can achieve this end by following precisely the way of life which Jesus taught.

Putting "on the new self" begins with genuine honesty with ourselves and with others, especially with the Lord. Jesus says: "Learn from me, for I am meek and humble of heart" (Mt 11:29).

19 *And this is the promise that he made us: eternal life.* (1 Jn 2:25)

When Jesus willingly laid down his life for us, it was much more than an expiatory sacrifice to atone for our sins. By his resurrection he created an exalted, glorified new life which he can now share with us.

Jesus took our human nature down to death with him, so that we could also rise with him triumphantly. When he redeemed our fallen nature, he gave us the capacity to receive his divine life and love.

The eternal life which he promised us is a sharing in the love, peace, and joy of the life of the Holy Trinity.

All praise, honor, and glory be to you, Lord Jesus!

20 *. . . "This is my body, which will be given for you; do this in memory of me."* . . . *"This cup is the new covenant in my blood, which will be shed for you."* (Lk 22:19-20)

Jesus instituted the Holy Eucharist to remain with us in a tangible form that we could more easily comprehend. He created his Eucharistic Presence to assure us of his abiding presence. In the Eucharist Jesus can assist and encourage, comfort and console, and give us strength and hope as our daily companion through all the ups and downs of daily living.

In his boundless love, he could not separate himself from us. He expressed this longing when he said: "I have eagerly desired to eat this Passover with you." He says the same to us each time we meet him in the Eucharistic celebration.

Lord, give us that same longing for you in the Eucharist.

HOLY SPIRIT

21 *The LORD God formed man out of the clay of the ground and blew into his nostrils the breath of life, and so man became a living being.*
(Gn 2:7)

Every person is a masterpiece of God's creative love. The Lord endowed every one with the "breath of life." In his great love for us our gracious Father didn't just provide us with physical life, he also found a way to share with us his own divine life. He gave us the very source of divine life, his Holy Spirit.

Just as physical life means growth, change, and development; our spiritual life also must grow, mature, and transform us.

Thank you, Lord, for the gift of life. Please help us attain eternal life with you in the bliss of heaven.

22 *Now Joshua, son of Nun, was filled with the spirit of wisdom, since Moses had laid his hands upon him; . . .* (Dt 34:9)

The Holy Spirit's gift of wisdom is not so much an accumulation of knowledge, but rather the insights we need to recognize the action of God in our lives. Wisdom teaches us how to live that we might attain the happiness and peace which the Lord wants us to enjoy in life.

This gift of the Spirit equipped Joshua to assume the guidance and direction of the chosen people when Moses died. The Holy Spirit likewise teaches us how to act and react in every situation. He does so without our even being conscious of it at times. He shows us how to avoid sin:

> Happy the man who follows not
>   the counsel of the wicked
> Nor walks in the way of sinners,
>   nor sits in the company of the insolent.
>   (Ps 1:1)

23 *"Let your every creature serve you; / for you spoke, and they were made, / You sent forth your spirit, and they were created; / no one can resist your word."* (Jdt 16:14)

In her fervent prayer, saintly and courageous Judith praised God for the gift of life and prayed fervently for the Lord to protect the lives of herself and her people.

O Spirit of God, I thank you for not only creating us, but also for giving us the mind and will to want to serve you.

Today, we offer every task and duty in our daily routine as a loving service to you. Please accept what we do with all its imperfections and shortcomings as a love-offering to you.

24 For the spirit of God has made me, / the breath of the Almighty keeps me alive.

(Jb 33:4)

The great tragedies of losing his sons and daughters in death and his own dreadful physical suffering and humiliation brought Job to a deeper awareness of God's inscrutable plans in his life.

He recognized God's almighty power as the source of life and his providential love for keeping his people alive day after day.

Disappointments, tragedies, pain, and suffering can have diverse effects on us. They can produce a rebellious heart toward God, or they can bring us to a richer appreciation of God's love veiled in mysterious ways in our lives.

Lord, give us the grace to recognize your caring love under any and all circumstances!

25 John answered them all, saying, "I am baptizing you with water, but one mightier than I is coming. . . . He will baptize you with the holy Spirit and fire." (Lk 3:16)

In its original usage, the word "baptism" means a total immersion or complete inundation. Jesus referred to his dreadful passion as a baptism with which he had to be baptized. This means he let himself be plunged into it completely.

When we were baptized in the Holy Spirit,

we were completely immersed into his divine life and love. Now his divine life overshadows us and fills us with a longing for the Lord's love and acceptance. He creates within us a desire for all that is good and holy. He gives us the will and determination to pursue a way of life which will lead us to our eternal union with him.

Come, Holy Spirit come! *Veni Sancte Spiritu!*

26 *"It is the spirit that gives life, while the flesh is of no avail. The words I have spoken to you are spirit and life."* (Jn 6:63)

The Holy Spirit adds an infinite dimension to our human life when, at baptism, he shares with us his divine life and love. We become totally immersed in his supernatural life.

This divine life within us is nurtured and increased through the Word of God spoken to us by Jesus. His Word was often misunderstood and rejected because his hearers, and many of us, could not fathom the deeply spiritual aspect of this unique heavenly gift—the Lord's indwelling.

Holy Spirit, grant us the wisdom and understanding to comprehend a little better your overwhelming love.

27 *For those who are led by the Spirit of God are children of God.* (Rom 8:14)

Our adoption as the children of God takes place at the moment of our baptism. At this moment, the Holy Spirit comes to abide with us, making us his special temple. This divine gift and privilege gives us our real dignity as members of the family of God.

Every privilege carries with it a responsibility. "Led by the Spirit" we are called to live a more deeply committed Christian way of life. The Holy Spirit gives us the motivation and courage to implement this way of life. He enlightens us with his gift of discernment to recognize the will of the Lord in all things.

Holy Spirit, grant us the grace to follow your leading.

28 *In him you also are being built together into a dwelling place of God in the Spirit.*
(Eph 2:22)

Jesus' redeeming love united us with the Father and sent the Holy Spirit to mold, shape, and transform us into a dwelling place for the Godhead. Thus Jesus fulfilled his promise: "Whoever loves me will keep my word, and my Father will love him, and we will come to him and make our dwelling with him" (Jn 14:23).

The love of God which is being poured into our hearts by the Holy Spirit will enable us to love our neighbor as ourselves, because the Spirit will help us recognize that our neighbor is also a dwelling place for the triune God.

Lord, may we recognize your dwelling place in everyone we meet each day.

29 *For in one Spirit we were all baptized into one body . . . and we were all given to drink of one Spirit.* (1 Cor 12:13)

Love, by its very nature, binds us together in a close union of minds and hearts. When we received the Holy Spirit in baptism, we immediately established some close relationships: the Father adopted us as his sons and daughters. Since we are all members of the family of God, we are in a real sense brothers and sisters to one another.

When "we were all given to drink of one Spirit," we receive an influx of his divine love that enables us to remove all barriers and strengthens the bond uniting us as members of the body of Christ.

Holy Spirit, continue to increase your love within us, that we may be able to enter into that community of perfect love with you and the Father and Son for all eternity.

30 *". . . I [am] the Alpha and the Omega, the beginning and the end. To the thirsty I will give a gift from the spring of life-giving water."*

(Rv 21:6)

We are the "thirsty" when we love God so much that we want to do everything which is pleasing to him. The Lord, pleased with our intention and desire, realizes that of ourselves we could not reach this end unless the Holy Spirit, the Sanctifier, is operative within us. He graciously sends us the Spirit—life-giving water—to assist us every moment of the day.

Come, Holy Spirit, endow us with all your gifts that we may live a fruitful life here in this land of exile and reach our eternal home with you.

HOLY TRINITY

31 *. . . The one who gives us security with you in Christ and who anointed us is God; he has also put his seal upon us and given the Spirit in our hearts as a first installment.* (2 Cor 1:21-22)

The creative love of God is clearly at work in this Trinitarian passage. The Father began the process of our initiation into the Christian life when he gave us his Son Jesus as our

Savior and Redeemer. After reconciling us with the Father, Jesus and the Father sent the Holy Spirit to carry out the work of our sanctification.

This whole process is the "first installment" of all the messianic benefits which have been promised to all who live the Christian way of life.

O Blessed Trinity, we praise, honor, and thank you as we say: Glory be to the Father, and to the Son, and to the Holy Spirit. Amen.

God's Love Provides

As each one has received a gift, use it to serve one another as good stewards of God's varied grace. (1 Pt 4:10)

FATHER

1 *For I know well the plans I have in mind for you, says the LORD, plans for your welfare, not for woe! plans to give you a future full of hope.*
(Jer 29:11)

Every minute detail of our life is planned or permitted by God for our welfare. Even though an experience may seem tragic and traumatic at the time, God can and does bring good out of it. Often we discover this after some time has elapsed.

Each one of life's experiences is a stepping stone into a deeper love-relationship with our benevolent Father.

With Mary as our exemplar, may our response always be: "May it be done to me according to your word" (Lk 1:38).

2 *He will give rain for the seed / that you sow in the ground, / And the wheat that the soil produces / will be rich and abundant....* (Is 30:23)

The rain, the sunshine, and all the climatic conditions for a rich harvest are gifts from our caring Father. Likewise the people who planted the seed, nurtured it, harvested it, transported it, and prepared it for our table are all provided by our provident Father.

In return, he asks only for our love, trust, and gratitude.

It is good to give thanks to the LORD,
   to sing praise to your name, Most High
To proclaim your kindness at dawn
   and your faithfulness throughout the
     night. (Ps 92:2-3)

3 *For your kindness towers to the heavens, / and your faithfulness to the skies. / Be exalted above the heavens, O God; / above all the earth be your glory!* (Ps 57:11-12)

The inspired writer's use of words such as "heavens" and "skies" assures us that there is absolutely no limit to the outpouring of the Father's kindness and faithfulness.

We express our gratitude and appreciation to him by loving and trusting our benevolent Father. May our hearts be lifted

up always to praise, honor, and glorify our
generous God.

With the psalmist we pray:

Let all your works give you thanks,
O LORD,
and let your faithful ones bless you.
(Ps 145:10)

4 *... He will be gracious to you when you cry
out, / as soon as he hears he will answer
you. / The Lord will give you the bread you need /
and the water for which you thirst....* (Is 30:19-20)

The providing love of the Father envelops
us at every moment of the day. He gives so
much—literally everything. We easily take
his generosity for granted.

We breathe in his life-giving oxygen over
twenty-five thousand times a day with only
a rare "thank you." The Lord wants us to
ask for all that we need, that we might
acknowledge him as our provider. Our asking also refines our petition. Our caring
Father awaits our "thank you."

Give thanks to the LORD, for he is good,
for his kindness endures forever!
(Ps 107:1)

5 ... *He bestows a greater grace; therefore, it says: / "God resists the proud, / but gives grace to the humble."* (Jas 4:6)

Pride gives us a feeling of self-sufficiency. It causes us to depend more on our own gifts and talents and to rely less on God. God does not "resist the proud" by choice, but because the proud person is not receptive to his grace.

In contrast, the humble recognize that every gift comes from God, even down to their next pulse beat. Consequently, they are more receptive to his gifts and graces. God cannot curb his generosity to those who humbly recognize their need of him.

Jesus paused in his teaching to pray: "I give praise to you, Father, Lord of heaven and earth, for although you have hidden these things from the wise and learned you have revealed them to the childlike" (Mt 11:25).

6 *"If God so clothes the grass of the field, which grows today and is thrown into the oven tomorrow, will he not much more provide for you, O you of little faith?"* (Mt 6:30)

This teaching of Jesus leaves no room for undue worry or anxiety. Jesus asks for a total trust and confidence in the Father's providing love. Any excessive concern on our part about what we need, or what could happen to us, is due to a lack of faith in God.

Repeatedly, Jesus asked for a deeper faith in the Father and also in himself and in what he taught. When Jesus says "O you of little faith," it is not so much a criticism, but a plea for a more trusting faith. As confidence in God increases, worry subsides.

> Trust in the LORD and do good,
>   that you may dwell in the land and enjoy security. (Ps 37:3)

7 *"Instead, seek his kingdom, and these other things will be given you besides."* (Lk 12:31)

Jesus advises us to seek the kingdom of God to allay our fears and anxieties about a multitude of things of lesser importance. At the same time he promises to provide for all our cares and concerns. If we keep our focus on the Lord and our eternal destiny, many of the concerns which plague us now will become peripheral. Keeping our focus on the Lord will also help us acquire a more cosmic view and set our priorities in order.

Pray earnestly: "Thy kingdom come."

8 *The LORD will guard you from all evil; / he will guard your life. / The LORD will guard your coming and your going, / both now and forever.* (Ps 121:7-8)

Our own insecurity keeps us fearful of failure, worried about rejection, anxious about the unknown. All this in spite of the fact that the Lord assures us that he is our Father guarding our coming and our going. His abiding presence proves his loving acceptance of us as we are. A deeper awareness of his unconditional love for us will be the source of peace, joy, and happiness, leaving no room for fear in our lives.

"There is no fear in love, but perfect love drives out fear . . ." (1 Jn 4:18).

9 *O LORD, your kindness reaches to heaven; your faithfulness, to the clouds.* (Ps 36:6)

The psalmist had difficulty trying to express superlative concepts in his language. Instead he used lofty images to describe the boundless kindness and faithfulness of God.

Kindness and faithfulness are only a part of the all-embracive umbrella of God's blessings and gifts, which overshadow us at all times.

Thank you and praise you, Father, for the loving care you give so graciously throughout every hour of the day. May our hearts overflow with gratitude always.

10 *For we know that if our earthly dwelling, a tent, should be destroyed, we have a building from God, a dwelling not made with hands, eternal in heaven.* (2 Cor 5:1)

Life on earth is only temporary. We are on our journey through this land of exile to our eternal home. We desperately cling to this life on earth because we cannot imagine the utter joy, peace, and happiness which await us in our dwelling with the Lord.

We fear death because we are often plagued with an unworthiness syndrome. This anxiety is unnecessary, since the Holy Spirit assures us: "God, who is rich in mercy, because of the great love he had for us, even when we were dead in our transgressions, brought us to life with Christ . . . raised us up with him, and seated us with him in the heavens in Christ Jesus" (Eph 2:4-6). And the Spirit reemphasizes this thought one verse later: "By grace you have been saved through faith, and this is not from you; it is the gift of God" (Eph 2:8).

Thank you, Lord, for your love, mercy, and compassion.

SON

11 *"I have given you a model to follow, so that as I have done for you, you should also do."* (Jn 13:15)

Jesus not only taught us the way to our eternal destiny by giving us guidelines and directives for our Christian living, but he himself lived every detail of it to an eminent degree. His lifestyle is our model. We could well paraphrase Paul's classic definition of love and apply it to Jesus.

"Jesus is patient, Jesus is kind. He is not jealous, not pompous, he is not inflated, he is not rude, he does not seek his own interests, he is not quick-tempered, he does not brood over injury, he does not rejoice over wrong-doing but rejoices with the truth. He bears all things, believes all things, hopes all things, endures all things" (1 Cor 13:4-7, paraphrased).

12 *... Jesus stood up and exclaimed, "Let anyone who thirsts come to me and drink. Whoever believes in me, as scripture says: 'Rivers of living water will flow from within him.'"*

(Jn 7:37-38)

Like our Father, Jesus is a provident God supplying us with everything we need, especially the gift of his divine life, which he calls "living water." Jesus confers this "living water" when he pours his Spirit upon us through the sacraments.

This divine life should radiate through us, his disciples, to everyone who crosses our path: family, fellow workers, friends, casual acquaintances, and even strangers.

Lord, replenish me abundantly that I may be a river of living water for you!

13 *"I give you a new commandment: love one another. As I have loved you, so you also should love one another."* (Jn 13:34)

Jesus did not give us a new commandment to restrict our relationship with others or to curtail our freedom. This requirement to love as he loved is a necessary condition for us to live a happy, peaceful life in this world and to prepare for the fullness of life in the next.

Loving our neighbor may seem difficult or even impossible at times, but Jesus showed us the way. He showed us by his own example of how to even love our enemies. He sent the Holy Spirit to fill us with his love so that we could obey this challenging commandment. And the ideal we are to attain:

"As I have loved you, so you also should love one another."

14 *"... 'The kingdom of heaven is at hand.'... Without cost you have received; without cost you are to give."* (Mt 10:7-8)

We have become members of the household of God and have been introduced into his kingdom without any merit on our part. Jesus reminds us that we have received without cost and asks us to give without cost.

As Christians we are on center stage throughout life. Our words, attitudes, and actions all reflect our personal relationship with the Lord. We always influence others, whether we are aware of it or not. We may never know how the Lord uses us to draw others to himself.

Lord Jesus, I count on your presence and your power to enable me to give without cost.

15 *"No one has greater love than this, to lay down one's life for one's friends."* (Jn 15:13)

Jesus wanted to give us a deeper understanding of his unfathomable love for us when he said: "No one has greater love than this." His love for us was so intense that it prompted him to lay down his life willingly to gain our redemption. What greater proof do we need to know that he loves us? What more could he have given?

Jesus reminds us of his infinite love to dispel any fear or anxiety we may have about not being worthy or lovable. He did so also to encourage us to respond even more generously to his love.

Jesus, may your love spur us on to greater heights.

16 *Then Jesus took the loaves, gave thanks, and distributed them to those who were reclining, and also as much of the fish as they wanted.* (Jn 6:11)

Jesus' tender heart was deeply moved when he perceived how reluctant the people were to leave him to find rest and food which they needed urgently. Their desire to hear more of the message of the good news gave him the opportunity to demonstrate his providential love for them.

His prayerful preparation of offering thanks and the miraculous multiplication of the loaves and fish proved his loving concern. This was the ideal occasion for him to demonstrate his continual care and concern by promising them the gift of himself in the Eucharist.

"I am the bread of life; whoever comes to me will never hunger, and whoever believes in me will never thirst" (Jn 6:35).

17 ... *"This is my body that is for you. Do this in remembrance of me."* (1 Cor 11:24)

Jesus is always present with us in his glorified life, but since our thinking is so practical and pragmatic, we can neither fully appreciate nor always be aware of his spiritual presence. For this reason, he gave us himself in the Holy Eucharist under the tangible signs of bread and wine.

These elements, food and drink, remind us that he remains with us to accompany and strengthen us on our journey through life. They are also a constant reminder of the intensity of his love which cannot allow us to be separated from him. What greater gift could he have given us?

O Sacrament most holy,
  O Sacrament divine,
All praise and all thanksgiving
  be every moment thine!

18 *"This is why the Father loves me, because I lay down my life in order to take it up again. No one takes it from me, but I lay it down on my own. ..."* (Jn 10:17-18)

Jesus gave his life freely and willingly for our salvation. By his redemptive death, he reunited us with the Godhead. This total oblation of himself proved his caring, concerned love. Love gives in proportion to its depth. Infinite love cannot be fulfilled until it has given everything. That is why Jesus could lay down his life so willingly, in spite of the dreadful suffering involved in that giving.

By his death and resurrection he is now able to share his divine life with us. He shares this life partially here on earth and in fullness when we reach our home with him in heaven. He himself said: "I came so that they might have life and have it more abundantly" (Jn 10:10).

We can respond to this free gift of his life as joyfully as Paul did: "I live, no longer I, but Christ lives in me" (Gal 2:20).

19 *When Jesus saw his mother and the disciple there whom he loved, he said to his mother, "Woman, behold, your son."* (Jn 19:26)

Mary is rightly called the mother of the church since Jesus gave her to us, his disciples. Jesus is the head of his body, the church, while Mary is its heart.

A mother is a model for all her children. A mother's influence is usually powerful and permanent. Mary's life of loving commitment is a challenge to all of us. Her lifestyle is an ideal example for us to follow.

At the wedding feast in Cana, Jesus manifested the power of his mother's intercession. Mary continues her role as intercessor for us, her spiritual children. Her motherly advice to us would be the same as her direction to the attendants at the wedding in Cana: "Do whatever he tells you" (Jn 2:5).

20 *The dead man sat up and began to speak, and Jesus gave him to his mother.* (Lk 7:15)

In the culture of that day, the Gospel's brief statement, "the only son of his mother, and she was a widow," could have implied a lifetime of disgrace and rejection for this poor widow. If a family died out, it was considered to be a punishment from God. This meant that the surviving widow would not be accepted among her people.

Jesus' words to her, "Do not weep," revealed the empathy and pity of his loving heart. How his heart rejoiced as he restored life and health to her deceased son!

Jesus might have been thinking of his own dear mother, for he, the only Son of a widowed mother, would soon be taken from her.

HOLY SPIRIT

21 *"But I tell you the truth, it is better for you that I go. For if I do not go, the Advocate will not come to you. But if I go, I will send him to you."* (Jn 16:7)

Jesus sent the Holy Spirit to enlighten and guide us through the dark valleys of life. His coming is like the beginning of a new day. When the first streaks of dawn appear in the east, the darkness gradually begins to fade until the rising sun dispels it all with its brilliant rays.

Our journey through life is often shrouded in the darkness of fear, doubt, or lack of clear direction. The Holy Spirit is the divine light illuminating our way, if we listen with all our heart to his inspirations.

He asks only our trust.

22 *... The love of God has been poured out into our hearts through the holy Spirit that has been given us.* (Rom 5:5)

The Holy Spirit does not simply give us his precious gift of love; he dwells with us and acts within us as the very source of divine love. He makes us his temple so that he can abide with us always. This gives us our real dignity as a person and as a Christian.

He continues to fill us with his divine love so that we are able to reach out in loving concern for others. We are a sort of channel through which his love flows to all we meet.

What joy this truth brings us: that we are loved and lovable regardless of who we are or what we might have done!

Come, O Holy Spirit, and stay with us always.

23 *And when he had said this, he breathed on them and said to them, "Receive the holy Spirit. Whose sins you forgive are forgiven them, and whose sins you retain are retained."*

(Jn 20:22-23)

The fruits of redemption are supplied to us personally through the Holy Spirit, our Sanctifier. Jesus' atonement for sin is infinite. It is universal, and we are included in his redemption. Yet Jesus was aware that his forgiveness would sometimes seem too universal, too general, and would cause us to wonder whether or not we are included.

To allay our doubts and fear, Jesus conferred the Holy Spirit upon the apostles as he instituted the Sacrament of Reconciliation. Now, through the action of the Spirit in the sacrament, we can encounter Jesus and experience his forgiveness personally.

Thank you, Lord, for your peace and pardon conveyed through your Holy Spirit.

24 *Thanks be to God for his indescribable gift!* (2 Cor 9:15)

God's indescribable gift is his divine presence with us through the action of the Holy Spirit. He endows us with the gift of faith that we might believe and receive him as our Divine guest.

He fills us with his infinite love that we might be able to fulfill the ministry to which he has called us; wisdom to know and understand his call and inspirations; courage and strength to undertake our work; perseverance to remain faithful.

For this indescribable gift, we thank you.

25 *There are different kinds of spiritual gifts but the same Spirit; there are different forms of service but the same Lord.* (1 Cor 12:4-5)

The Lord calls every one of us to a particular vocation and to a special ministry within that vocation. He does not call us and leave us alone to fend for ourselves. Jesus' gift of the Holy Spirit equips us with every gift and grace, with every talent and ability we need to fulfill our mission in life.

In order to fulfill our call to love our neighbor as ourselves, the Spirit calls us to "different forms of service." With the gifts and help of the Holy Spirit, and with our own dedicated response, the body of Christ

will grow and mature as we journey together to our eternal destiny.

Praise you, Lord, for every gift you have
given us!

26 *But one and the same Spirit produces all of these, distributing them individually to each person as he wishes.* (1 Cor 12:11)

Even though we are all members of the
family of God, each of us has a distinct per-
sonality and temperament. To every member
the Holy Spirit gives the particular gifts he
or she needs for his or her ministry and for
"building up the body of Christ" (Eph 4:12).

The call to holiness is a universal call. The
Spirit equips each one of us with the special
gifts we require to persevere in our efforts.
Above all, he pours his love upon us to
motivate us in striving sincerely for that
goal.

Come, Holy Spirit, come.

27 *Do not neglect the gift you have, which was conferred on you through the prophetic word with the imposition of hands of the presbyterate.* (1 Tm 4:14)

St. Peter reminds us that we are "a chosen
race, a royal priesthood," since through
baptism we share in the priesthood of
Christ. Paul cautions us not to neglect the
gift we have received.

We use this privileged gift each time we join our eternal high priest along with the ordained priest at Mass to offer ourselves and all that we do to our loving Father. Our oblation touches the throne of God, thanks to the gift of the Holy Spirit.

May we always "worship the Father in Spirit and truth" (Jn 4:23).

28 *For this reason, I remind you to stir into flame the gift of God that you have through the imposition of my hands.* (2 Tm 1:6)

St. Paul was a dynamic spiritual guide. He understood our human weakness and complacency. He reminds us, as he did Timothy, not to neglect the special gifts and graces which the Holy Spirit so generously conferred upon us through the imposition of hands, especially at baptism and confirmation.

It would be most profitable for us to set aside a few moments each day to thank the Lord for one or more of the gifts we have received. As we recall the Spirit's many gifts, on a daily basis, our gratitude will grow. We will become even more zealous in using well all the gifts we have received.

Thank you, Father, for the gift of life.
Thank you, Jesus, for your gift of redemption.
Thank you, Holy Spirit, for your abiding, sanctifying presence.

29 ... *"What eye has not seen, and ear has not heard, / and what has not entered the human heart, / what God has prepared for those who love him," / this God has revealed to us through the Spirit. . . .* (1 Cor 2:9-10)

Since "we do not know how to pray as we ought," the Holy Spirit leads us into prayer, especially the prayer of the heart, by helping us listen with our whole being. This method of prayer gives us insights far beyond our reasoning powers.

The Holy Spirit creates within us a yearning, a longing, a desire for eternal happiness, even though our human mind cannot comprehend the peace and joy, the love and fulfillment which awaits us. We cannot possibly imagine "what God has prepared for those who love him."

St. Augustine tells us that the very desire we have for heaven is itself genuine prayer.

30 *The Spirit and the bride say, "Come." Let the hearer say, "Come." Let the one who thirsts come forward, and the one who wants it receive the gift of life-giving water.* (Rv 22:17)

The Lord never forces himself upon us, but he waits patiently for us to invite him into our lives. The Spirit invites us to come to the source of life-giving water. The church, the bride, also says "Come."

How eagerly the Lord awaits our response. He wants to walk with us through

the labyrinthine ways of life and guide us
safely to our home in heaven where we can
enjoy the life-giving water of his boundless
love.

"Come, Lord Jesus!"

HOLY TRINITY

31 *"Go, therefore, and make disciples of all
nations, baptizing them in the name of the
Father, and of the Son, and of the holy Spirit,
teaching them to observe all that I have commanded
you. . . ."* (Mt 28:19-20)

All three persons of the Blessed Trinity
have graciously provided us with countless
gifts and blessings. These were given us, in
the first place, for our own growth in holiness. They were also bestowed to make the
Lord better known and loved by others.
Scripture asserts that we received these gifts
"to equip the holy ones for the work of
ministry, for building up the body of Christ"
(Eph 4:12).

The Lord commissions us to reach out to
those who do not know him and strive to
lead them closer to him. We may hesitate to
reflect God's love and concern for them or to
speak about him to others. Yet Jesus allays
our fears when he assures us: "And behold, I
am with you always, until the end of the
age" (Mt 28:20).

Trinitarian Love
Forgives and Forgets

. . . Let us confidently approach the throne of grace to receive mercy . . . (Heb 4:16)

FATHER

1 *. . . With age-old love I have loved you; so I have kept my mercy toward you.* (Jer 31:3)

When we recall that God's love for us is immutable, unconditional, infinite, it staggers our imagination. We simply cannot comprehend it. His mercy, an integral part of his boundless love, will never change. Only we change. We can be wide open to God's mercy, or, God forbid, we can close it off by willful, unrepentant sin.

The Lord's mercy is just another dimension of his eternal love. His love manifested itself already in the Garden of Eden. Even though his creatures refused to love, the

121

Lord, nevertheless, promised them a Redeemer.

We praise and thank you, Father, for your age-old love.

2 *. . . All, from least to greatest, shall know me, says the LORD, for I will forgive their evil-doing and remember their sin no more.* (Jer 31:34)

When our loving Father has forgiven us, we experience an interior peace and joy which no other source can supply. This experiential awareness of his merciful love enables us to know the Lord not only intellectually, but with our heart. We recognize him as our compassionate Father. We may not be able to comprehend the depths of his kindness—in response to our waywardness—since it springs from his infinite love, which is too profound for us to understand.

Yet as our awareness of his infinite love grows, it will deter us more and more from sin.

Thank you, Lord, for forgetting.

3 *Forgive your people their sins and all the offenses they have committed against you, and grant them mercy before their captors, so that these will be merciful to them.* (1 Kgs 8:50)

In his prayer for his people, Solomon prayed that God's mercy would prevail in spite of the sinfulness of his people. Solomon was asking the Lord to create the proper disposition in his people, so that they could be in a position to receive the Lord's generous mercy and forgiveness.

Our gracious Father knows that most of our sins are committed out of human weakness, with no malicious intent. In our self-centeredness we prefer our own will to the will of God. We subordinate the love we should have for God to our love of self. Our own desires take precedence over what the Lord wishes for us.

Lord, help us practice what we pray: "Thy will be done."

4 *It is I, I, who wipe out, for my own sake, your offenses; your sins I remember no more.*

(Is 43:25)

How could the Lord say that he is wiping out our offenses and sins for his own sake? We must remember that the Lord loves us with an infinite love, and love must give in proportion to the depth of love.

Giving and forgiving is an integral part of genuine love. Since forgiveness is so personal, this facet of divine love brings us into a more profound appreciation of the immensity of his unconditional love. What joy we bring to the heart of our compassionate Father when we humbly and trustingly beg his forgiveness!

With the tax collector let us pray: "O God, be merciful to me a sinner" (Lk 18:13).

5 *... Fear not, for I have redeemed you; / I have called you by name: you are mine.* (Is 43:1)

God, our loving and gracious Father, in baptism you called us by name and confirmed your purpose for us. Even before our natural father could accept us and name us, you knew us perfectly. You adopted us and welcomed us into your heavenly family. As we ponder this tremendous mystery of your love, our hearts rejoice with praise and thanksgiving.

Your reassuring words remove all fear and anxiety which may cause our hearts to doubt your forgiveness. With your grace, help us to recognize the marvelous dignity you have conferred on us.

"Teach me to do your will, / for you are my God. / May your good spirit guide me / on level ground" (Ps 143:10).

6 *Do I indeed derive any pleasure from the death of the wicked? says the Lord GOD. Do I not rather rejoice when he turns from his evil way that he may live?* (Ez 18:23)

All too often, we have thought of the God of the Old Testament as a vengeful, punishing God to be feared. Unfortunately this notion has often obliterated his mercy and compassion. He himself tells us how much he rejoices when we turn to him in sorrow and sincerity that he may forgive us.

As we prayerfully reflect on what he tells us about himself in Scripture, we will come to appreciate his forgiving, compassionate heart. He assures us that he forgives us for his own sake, since his love is so great.

Lord, show us your mercy and kindness all the days of our lives.

7 *Answer me, O LORD, for bounteous is your kindness; / in your great mercy turn toward me.* (Ps 69:17)

How true is the adage: to err is human, to forgive is divine. Throughout his Word, our good God expresses repeatedly his eagerness to forgive us if we approach him with the right dispositions—recognizing the malice of sin, acknowledging our own faults, and humbly asking his pardon and peace.

In this prayer, the psalmist leads us into the proper dispositions. He does not try to hide his folly and faults from the Lord, but admits them and begs his merciful forgiveness. His disposition is pleasing to the Lord since it springs from a faith that the Father is bounteous in kindness and wants to show mercy to him.

Father, create in us humble, sincere, sorrowful hearts.

8 *"Listen in heaven and forgive the sin of your servants and of your people Israel. . . ."*

(2 Chr 6:27)

As people of the new Israel, we can make this prayer of Solomon our own plea for mercy and forgiveness, and we can be certain that our compassionate Father is listening. He listens not so much to our words, but to the dispositions of our hearts. Do we recognize sin as a refusal to love? Are we genuinely sorry and willing to strive to avoid sin in our lives?

If we are humbly sincere, we can be certain that the heart of our compassionate Father rejoices in not only forgiving our sins, but in forgetting them as well.

Thank you, Father, for the many times you have forgiven us.

9 *Those whom the LORD has ransomed will return . . . / crowned with everlasting joy; They will meet with joy and gladness, sorrow and mourning will flee.* (Is 51:11)

This prophecy promises the many blessings which the Redeemer will bring to the world. Jesus fulfilled this prophecy when he said that he came "to give his life as a ransom for many" (Mk 10:45).

The awareness of his redeeming love is the source of the joy and gladness we experience in this life as a prelude to the "everlasting joy" which awaits us in heaven.

> Happy is he whose fault is taken away,
>   whose sin is covered.
> Happy the man to whom the LORD
>   imputes not guilt,
>   in whose spirit there is no guile.
>
> (Ps 32:1-2)

10 *For God so loved the world that he gave his only Son, so that everyone who believes in him might not perish but might have eternal life.* (Jn 3:16)

The Father's love for us is so intense that he gave us the greatest gift he could give us—the gift of himself in the person of Jesus. He wants our eternal salvation more than we could want it ourselves.

As we contemplate this truth we can better appreciate all the love, mercy, compassion, forgiveness, and healing flowing from the heart of our gracious Father.

Father, we do believe, help us to believe even more fervently!

SON

11 *"I am the good shepherd, and I know mine and mine know me, just as the Father knows me and I know the Father; and I will lay down my life for the sheep."* (Jn 10:14-15)

As the Good Shepherd, Jesus loves and cares for all the needs of his sheep. In this touching metaphor Jesus reveals the extent of his sacrificial love for us. He exercised this love to obtain our greatest need—redemption. He willingly laid down his life that we "might have life and have it more abundantly" (Jn 10:10).

Jesus also reminds us: "No one has greater love than this, to lay down one's life for one's friends" (Jn 15:13). The very day after Jesus spoke these words, he laid down his life for us.

Lord, keep us always docile, trusting, grateful sheep.

12 *He delivered us from the power of darkness and transferred us to the kingdom of his beloved Son, in whom we have redemption, the forgiveness of sins.* (Col 1:13-14)

I once asked a priest-friend of mine why a mutual acquaintance always looked so sad and unhappy. His answer was immediate, and I believe, accurate. He replied: "He does not know that he is redeemed.''

As we ponder this situation, it will make us appreciate the Lord's gift of faith to us and also the peace and joy which we experience in knowing our sins are forgiven and that our own resurrection is a divine promise.

May our peace and joy radiate to all those who do not know that they are redeemed.

13 . . . *"Neither do I condemn you. Go, [and] from now on do not sin any more."*

(Jn 8:11)

The forgiving love of Jesus was put to the test when the scribes and Pharisees brought the adulterous woman to him to trap him. If he excused her, he would be denying the law of Moses. If he condemned her, he would be nullifying his teaching on forgiveness. Jesus was not to be ensnared in their vicious plot.

Apparently Jesus let her accusers know that they too, were sinful men. Unlike the woman, they chose to leave and avoid Jesus rather than turn from their self-righteousness and accept forgiveness.

The forgiving love of the Lord is eternal. No sin is too great to receive divine forgiveness, if the sinner is truly repentant and resolves to avoid sin to the best of his or her ability. St. Paul reminds us: "where sin

increased, grace overflowed all the more"
(Rom 5:20).

> A clean heart create for me, O God,
>   and a steadfast spirit renew within me.
> (Ps 51:12)

14 *In him we have redemption by his blood, the forgiveness of transgressions, in accord with the riches of his grace.* (Eph 1:7)

By his suffering and death, Jesus not only freed us from the punishment due to our sins, but he also redeemed our fallen human nature. He restored to us the ability to receive his divine life which he shares with us. This divine life is the antecedent of our own resurrection into glory. We are a privileged people.

St. Paul's words are so reaffirming:

> We were indeed buried with him through baptism into death, so that, just as Christ was raised from the dead by the glory of the Father, we too might live in newness of life. (Rom 6:4)

Lord, may we celebrate the joy of the resurrection all the days of our life.

15 *"Go and learn the meaning of the words, 'I desire mercy, not sacrifice.' I did not come to call the righteous but sinners."* (Mt 9:13)

Since it was the Pharisees who pretended to be shocked that he associated with sinners, Jesus quoted a prophet whom they knew: "It is love that I desire, not sacrifice" (Hos 6:6). Jesus was trying to impress on them that loving forgiveness superseded their ceremonial laws. Their words and actions were empty when not performed with the right dispositions.

Jesus came as Savior to redeem our sinful human nature. He came to extend mercy and forgiveness to all who could receive him and believe in him. Jesus set forth some clear-cut instructions on judging others.

"Why do you notice the splinter in your brother's eye, but do not perceive the wooden beam in your own eye? ... remove the wooden beam from your eye first; then you will see clearly to remove the splinter from your brother's eye" (Mt 7:3, 5).

Jesus, thank you for your pointed admonition.

16 *He said to her, "Your sins are forgiven."* (Lk 7:48)

In this Gospel episode, Jesus is confronting two sinners with very diverse dispositions—a sinful woman in the city and a proud, self-righteous Pharisee. The sinful woman was filled with sorrow and repentance, therefore her forgiveness was immediate. We are not certain about the forgiveness of the Pharisee.

Jesus deals with us in the same way. Sinfulness poses no problem if we come to him with sorrow, repentance, and the resolve to try to serve him more faithfully. His love is a forgiving, healing love always available to us if we are receptive. His mercy and compassion are inexhaustible.

"... A heart contrite and humbled, O God, you will not spurn" (Ps 51:19).

17 *"If you forgive others their transgressions, your heavenly Father will forgive you. But if you do not forgive others, neither will your Father forgive your transgressions."* (Mt 6:14-15)

Jesus gave us the golden rule as a guideline for many areas of our daily living. "Do to others whatever you would have them do to you" (Mt 7:12).

One of the areas where we can apply this maxim is in forgiving others when they have offended us. Jesus makes this a condition for us to receive his forgiveness.

We have experienced the peace which fills our heart when the Lord forgives us all our faults and failings. We also know joy and relief after a friend or loved one forgives us when we have hurt them. Our first step to obtaining the Lord's forgiveness is to forgive anyone who has offended us. For this grace we pray:

"Forgive us our trespasses as we forgive those who trespass against us."

18 *"Whose sins you forgive are forgiven them, and whose sins you retain are retained."*
(Jn 20:23)

We, the members of the body of Christ, are being purified and sanctified by the Holy Spirit as we journey toward our eternal destiny. On our journey we support and encourage one another. We also channel the Lord's love and life to all who travel with us. However, when we sin, we deprive other members of God's family of the love and grace which should be flowing through us.

When we receive the Sacrament of Reconciliation, our sinfulness is taken away and once again we can share the divine gifts with one another. This sacramental rite reinstates us as dedicated disciples of the Lord reaching out to all our brothers and sisters.

Lord, let us hear your gracious words: "Your sins are forgiven."

19 *Then Jesus said, "Father, forgive them, they know not what they do."* . . . (Lk 23:34)

Even in his final agonizing moments, Jesus continued to prove his boundless love. In spite of the dreadful pain, he was not thinking about himself, but about his enemies and us as well. He not only asked the Father to forgive us and them, but he even excused us, "they know not what they do."

Pondering these words will not only dispose us to be receptive to his forgiving love, but it will also deter us from further sinful turning away from him. Jesus knows our humanness and how prone we are to indulge our own sinful nature, hence he excuses us. We can be certain that he is always eager to forgive us at any time.

Jesus, keep my heart humble, contrite, and docile.

20 . . . *"Amen, I say to you, today you will be with me in Paradise."* (Lk 23:43)

The cross of Jesus is a study in contrasts. While it displays the inhumanity of man, it also reveals the contrasting goodness of the Lord. In contrast to the hatred, ridicule, and blasphemy leveled at Jesus, his comforting words to the criminal touch our hearts profoundly, revealing the mystery of divine mercy and love.

When the criminal asked Jesus just to be remembered when he came into his king-

dom, Jesus did not reproach him with the
crimes which led to his execution, nor did he
exact any kind of admission of sorrow. Jesus
recognized the disposition of the man's
heart and promised the criminal that they
would be united in heaven that very day.
The criminal stole heaven as his final act.

Lord Jesus, we pray that we may hear the
same reassuring words when the time of our
death approaches.

HOLY SPIRIT

21 *Now the Lord is the Spirit, and where the
Spirit of the Lord is, there is freedom.*
(2 Cor 3:17)

The Holy Spirit is the source of genuine
freedom. He enlightens and guides us along
the path leading us to the Father. He helps
us discern the will of the Lord and gives us
the courage and motivation to conform our
lives to it.

If we should have the misfortune to fall
into sin and thus lose our freedom, the Holy
Spirit will gently lead us into sorrow and
repentance and on into forgiveness and
healing. When Jesus empowered his first
priests to forgive sins, he did so through the
infusion of the Holy Spirit: "Receive the holy
Spirit. Whose sins you forgive are forgiven
them" (Jn 20:23).

Freedom is the fruit of forgiveness. With this freedom we will know the peace and joy which the Lord has in store for us.

22 *"But the hour is coming, and is now here, when true worshipers will worship the Father in Spirit and truth; and indeed the Father seeks such people to worship him."* (Jn 4:23)

Realizing that we are a redeemed people and led by the indwelling of the Holy Spirit, we can worship the Father with sincere, humble hearts and minds. Jesus lamented the strictly ceremonial ritual of his people which was often empty words. "This people honors me with their lips, / but their hearts are far from me" (Mt 15:8).

Genuine worship springs from an awe and reverence of the might and power of the transcendent God of heaven and earth. It is also a grateful recognition of God's infinite goodness, of the providing care and concern, of the forgiving, healing love of our gracious Father. Praise, honor, glory, and thanksgiving is our loving, worshipful response to our all-good God.

"We worship you, we give you thanks, we praise you for your glory" (Gloria of the Mass).

23 *... Now you have had yourselves washed, you were sanctified, you were justified in the name of the Lord Jesus Christ and in the Spirit of our God.* (1 Cor 6:11)

The Father accepted us into his family by virtue of our baptism in which we were justified through the redemptive merits of Jesus. Now the Holy Spirit continues to purify and sanctify us as we journey through our earthly exile preparing for our entry into glory.

This mystery of justification and sanctification is proof that the tremendous forgiving and healing love of the Lord is poured out upon us. We are special. We belong to him. He is living with us at every turn of the road. This privilege and dignity inspires us to live a life as blameless as possible. However, if we fail, we know that the Lord's forgiveness is held out to every humble, contrite heart.

Lord, be merciful to us sinners.

24 *A clean heart create for me, O God, / and a steadfast spirit renew within me. / Cast me not out from your presence, / and your holy spirit take not from me.* (Ps 51:12-13)

The special mission of the Holy Spirit dwelling within us is to enable us to detect the machinations of the evil one in times of temptation, to strengthen us against his onslaughts, to motivate us and lead us into holiness.

O Holy Spirit, never leave us, but continue to purify and sanctify us and transform us into the people you want us to be.

25 *. . . You were ransomed from your futile conduct, handed on by your ancestors, not with perishable things like silver or gold but with the precious blood of Christ as of a spotless unblemished lamb.* (1 Pt 1:18-19)

According to a Jewish tradition, blood was the symbol of life. When Jesus poured out his very last drop of blood for our redemption, he gave us a share in his divine life as a prelude to the fullness of divine life and love which awaits us in eternity.

Jesus handed over the final stage of our salvation to the Holy Spirit, who fills us with his divine love to encourage and motivate us along our trek heavenward. The Spirit inspires and guides us, he cautions and protects us, he comforts and consoles us as we journey along.

What more could have been done for us?

26 *Undeniably great is the mystery of devotion, / Who was manifested in the flesh, vindicated in the spirit, / seen by angels, / proclaimed to the Gentiles, / believed in throughout the world, taken up in glory.* (1 Tm 3:16)

Jesus is the visible mystery of divine love, mercy, and compassion. He took on our human nature that he might redeem us, making us capable of receiving his divine life and love. He died as a common criminal in order to justify us wayward sinners. He was vindicated by the Holy Spirit, and through this Spirit he continues the work of our sanctification.

As the Holy Spirit fills us with his divine love and life, we experience great peace and joy, knowing that his infinite love will not justify us, but that it will not rest until we are taken up with him in glory.

All you angels and saints rejoice with us and unite your thanks with ours as we praise the Lord for his redemptive love.

27 *"Therefore, I say to you, every sin and blasphemy will be forgiven people, but blasphemy against the Spirit will not be forgiven."*
(Mt 12:31)

Jesus was not declaring that the Holy Spirit's desire and power to forgive is limited. It means that a sinner who refuses to acknowledge his sinfulness, and who does not want forgiveness will not be forgiven by the Holy Spirit. God does not force himself upon us. He waits for our willingness to receive his forgiveness.

Come, O Holy Spirit, help us to acknowledge humbly and sincerely our sinfulness and always to be receptive to your forgiving, healing love.

28 *"... But if I go, I will send him to you. And when he comes he will convict the world in regard to sin and righteousness and condemnation."* (Jn 16:7-8)

One of the evils besetting society today is the fact that we have lost our sense of sin. The crisis in faith in God is accompanied by the rejection of his moral code. Some would have us believe that actions which were once considered personal sin are really only psychological needs which we fulfill as we try to become whole persons.

The Holy Spirit leads believers to understand sin basically as a refusal to love Jesus and the moral code he proposed for our happiness and well-being. He not only convicts us of sin, but leads us to sorrow, forgiveness, and into righteousness.

Come, Holy Spirit, and remain with us in this time of need.

29 *I say, then: live by the Spirit and you will certainly not gratify the desire of the flesh.* (Gal 5:16)

Our life is like a tug-of-war that draws us in opposite directions. Our broken human nature craves self-indulgence, which leads us far from the designated way of Jesus who is "the way and the truth and the life" (Jn 14:6). Such gratification ends in misery, frustration, and unhappiness.

Tugging in the opposite direction is the powerful grace of the Holy Spirit, who endows us with countless gifts and encourages us to follow his leading. He promises us his love, which is the embodiment of peace, joy, patience, kindness, and a whole host of other fruits.

Holy Spirit, help us to allow ourselves to be tugged in your direction and keep our focus ever fixed on the destiny you offer us.

30 *In your mercy you led the people you redeemed; / in your strength you guided them to your holy dwelling.* (Ex 15:13)

This brief excerpt from Moses' canticle gives a prophetic vision of the redemption by Jesus and the guidance of the Holy Spirit to our final dwelling place. This canticle celebrates the saving power of God, who miraculously freed his people from their enemies and led them to their victorious conquest of the Promised Land.

Moses' song is a prophecy and promise of Jesus, our Redeemer. It prefigures the way Jesus will break the power of our enemy, the devil, and the way the Holy Spirit will lead us toward our eternal Promised Land. Through the indwelling of the Holy Spirit we are forgiven and healed of our sinfulness and inspired as he leads us along the way to his "holy dwelling."

". . . I will sing to the LORD, for he is gloriously triumphant" (Ex 15:1).

HOLY TRINITY

31 *The Spirit itself bears witness with our spirit that we are children of God, and if children, then heirs, heirs of God and joint heirs with Christ, if only we suffer with him so that we may also be glorified with him.* (Rom 8:16-17)

Our gracious God assures us that the mercy, compassion, forgiveness, and healing shown us, is the ministration of all the three persons of the Blessed Trinity. The Father calls us to the cleansing waters of baptism in order to adopt us as his special children.

By laying down his life willingly, Jesus freed us from our sinfulness and made us heirs of his eternal kingdom. The Spirit continues this work of purification and sanctification within us throughout our lives.

Nothing can come between us and the life and love which God wants to share with us. Amen! Alleluia!

The Lord's Love Heals

. . . The LORD restores the well-being of his people. . . . (Ps 14:7)

FATHER

1 *". . . I, the LORD, am your healer."* (Ex 15:26)

The Lord assured the Israelites in the desert that he had healed them from many diseases which afflicted the Egyptians. His healing love hovered over them at all times.

We cannot possibly know from how many illnesses the Lord has spared us because of his healing love. Our repeated thanks for the gift of life, for good health, and for his enduring love, will be most pleasing to him. We will become remembering people, and this will make us grateful people.

2 *He sent forth his word to heal them / and to snatch them from destruction. / Let them give thanks to the LORD for his kindness / and his wondrous deeds to the children of men.* (Ps 107:20-21)

There is power in the Word of the Lord. The prophet assures us that when God sends out his Word, it does not return until it achieves the end for which he sent it (Is 55:11).

As we hear the Word of the Lord in the liturgy at Mass or in our personal prayer and permit it to find a home in our heart, we will experience a healing of our lack of loving concern for others and also a healing from many of our selfish tendencies.

3 ... *"Please, not this! Pray, heal her!"*
(Nm 12:13)

In order to transform the minds and hearts of the Israelites, God worked many signs and wonders to impress upon them his divine power.

God showed his displeasure when Miriam became jealous of Moses and permitted her suddenly to become a leper. Her equally sudden healing, at the prayer of Moses, proved God's loving concern as well as his power.

In today's crisis of faith, the Lord continues to work signs and wonders to strengthen our faith. Pray as Moses did, that his healing overshadow us at all times.

4 *Bless the LORD, O my soul; . . . / He pardons all your iniquities, / he heals all your ills. He redeems your life from destruction, / he crowns you with kindness and compassion.* (Ps 103:1, 3-4)

We often beg the Lord to pardon our iniquities and to forgive our sins without realizing that in some cases we may need healing more than forgiveness.

If we are constantly uncharitable to a certain person, it may be a symptom of an area where we need healing. We must be healed of whatever causes us to be unkind, be it jealousy, envy, insecurity, or resentment.

At all times bless the Lord for his compassion.

5 *I drew them with human cords, / with bands of love; / I fostered them like one who raises an infant to his cheeks; / Yet, though I stooped to feed my child, / they did not know that I was their healer.* (Hos 11:4)

Portraying himself as a loving Father, the Lord draws us to himself with the kindness and affection which a good father has for his child. Even though we may be oblivious to his loving concern for us, he will never give up on us nor abandon us.

Listen again to the words of the Lord. Could he be speaking about us? Do we remind ourselves continuously that he is our healer?

Thank you, Father, for your enduring love.

6 . . . *"O LORD, have pity on me; / heal me, though I have sinned against you."* (Ps 41:5)

The first step in seeking healing and forgiveness from the Lord is to recognize our sinfulness. Then we must acknowledge it honestly, and finally we should humbly and sincerely seek the Lord's forgiveness and healing.

Our loving Father never forces himself upon us, but he is overjoyed when we turn to him, regardless of what we have done. He is not only available at all times but is eagerly disposed to forgive and heal, if we ask him.

7 *Heal me, LORD, that I may be healed; / save me, that I may be saved, / for it is you whom I praise.* (Jer 17:14)

The prophet's prayer for healing provides a good example for us. When something vexes us and we find ourselves getting impatient or angry, disturbed or tense, anxious or worried, we can turn to the Lord with a simple prayer for healing: "Lord, Heal Me." Repeat this brief prayer any number of times until the irritant is gone.

Constant repetition of this prayer will help us form a habit pattern which will bring greater peace, serenity, and contentment into our lives.

8 *"I was sent to put you to the test. At the same time, however, God commissioned me to heal you and your daughter-in-law Sarah."* (Tb 12:14)

Many times God heals us directly without our even being aware of it. At other times he heals us through a mediator. In the beautiful love story of Tobiah, the Lord sent the angel Raphael to heal the elder Tobit of blindness and also to heal Sarah of the evil spirit operative in her life.

The Lord may empower us to be a healing balm to others by our prayers with them and for them and also by our very presence which radiates to them the Lord's love, peace, and joy.

9 *"I myself will pasture my sheep; I myself will give them rest, says the Lord GOD. The lost I will seek out, the strayed I will bring back, the injured I will bind up, the sick I will heal . . . shepherding them rightly."* (Ez 34:15-16)

The image of God as our Shepherd and we as the sheep of his flock brings us much joy and happiness. Our gracious Father not only reminds us that he is providing for and protecting us as the Good Shepherd, but also that he is healing all those areas where we are in need.

With confidence and trust let us heed his call, come to him, and let him heal us. The Lord does not impose himself on us, he waits for us.

10 *Praise the LORD, for he is good; / . . . He heals the brokenhearted / and binds up their wounds.* (Ps 147:1, 3)

The highway of life is strewn with many heartaches and disappointments. Some of these rejections are heart-rending and cause great pain. At times, family and friends can be of little comfort.

Fortunately our caring Father, the God of all comfort and consolation, is ever ready to heal us and reassure us with his boundless love.

Seek him out before turning to human comfort.

SON

11 *. . . "Go and tell John what you hear and see: the blind regain their sight, the lame walk, lepers are cleansed, the deaf hear, the dead are raised, and the poor have the good news proclaimed to them."* (Mt 11:4-5)

Jesus wanted to be known as a healer. He healed not so much to prove his divine power, as to manifest his loving care and concern for anyone who was suffering.

Jesus is equally concerned about us today. He heals us in countless different ways of which we may not be even aware, provided we are open and receptive to his healing love.

12 *Jesus stretched out his hand, touched him, and said, "I do will it. Be made clean." . . .*
(Lk 5:13)

Leprosy was a loathsome, terminal disease. It was the AIDS of Jesus' time. Lepers were confined to a leper colony separated from family and friends. They were erroneously considered grave sinners, which intensified their suffering.

The leper risked his life in seeking out Jesus. Jesus appreciated his faith and trust as his response indicates: "I do will it. Be made clean."

Jesus, thank you for healing me so often from the leprosy of sin.

13 *. . . "What do you want me to do for you?" The blind man replied to him, "Master, I want to see."* (Mk 10:51)

Jesus was deeply moved by the faith and perseverance of Bartimaeus, who kept calling out to him. He pleaded with Jesus: "Master, I want to see." With compassion Jesus reassured him: "Go your way; your faith has saved you."

We can make the blind man's prayer our own: "Master, I want to see." Lord, grant me the faith and perseverance to see, understand, and fulfill your will in my life.

14 ... *"Young man, I tell you, arise!"*
(Lk 7:14)

Did Jesus envision his own mother when he saw the weeping widow of Nain, whose only son was being carried out to be buried? His own death in the not-too-distant future would deprive his mother of her only Son.

This episode in the Gospel reveals the compassion and tenderness of the heart of Jesus as he says "Do not weep."

Jesus, bring comfort and consolation to all mothers, especially to those whose sons and daughters have strayed away from you and from them.

15 *So he was not able to perform any mighty deed there, apart from curing a few sick people by laying his hands on them. He was amazed at their lack of faith.* (Mk 6:5-6)

Jesus was amazed and deeply disappointed when the people of his hometown of Nazareth refused to believe in him and rejected him completely. They prevented him from showering untold blessings upon all of them.

When we place all our faith, confidence, and trust in the Lord, we can be certain that he will respond to our needs and guide and assist us in all of life's problems and perplexities.

May we never amaze Jesus by our lack of faith.

16 *When Jesus saw him lying there and knew that he had been ill for a long time, he said to him, "Do you want to be well?"* (Jn 5:6)

This may seem like a rather strange question for Jesus to ask of the ill man at the pool at the Sheep Gate. We must remember that only handicapped persons were permitted to beg for a living. Jesus wanted the man to realize that he would have to change his way of life if he were healed. Once again Jesus shows his sensitivity to all our needs.

When we ask Jesus for some special gift or favor, we may also have to be prepared to adjust our lifestyle in order to use the gift effectively.

17 *"Which is easier, to say to the paralytic, 'Your sins are forgiven,' or to say, 'Rise, pick up your mat and walk'?"* (Mk 2:9)

Jesus was very pleased when people believed in him. When they refused to believe in him, he was deeply disappointed.

The faith of the men who carried the paralytic pleased Jesus greatly. He also appreciated their herculean efforts to present the paralyzed man to him. Jesus did not hesitate to heal the whole person—physically, psychologically, and spiritually, even though he knew he would be criticized for doing so.

Lord, grant me the faith of these men who brought the paralytic to you.

18 *Jesus said in reply, "Ten were cleansed, were they not? Where are the other nine?"* (Lk 17:17)

All ten lepers were healed as Jesus sent them on their way, but only one returned to thank Jesus. Jesus was manifestly disappointed. The other nine probably rushed home to announce the good news.

We, too, can easily become so preoccupied with all the demands of daily living that we may not take time to tell the Lord how grateful we are for his countless blessings.

It would be profitable to jot down each day three or four blessings that we have received. It would help us become even more grateful people.

19 . . . *"Stop, no more of this!" Then he touched the servant's ear and healed him.*
(Lk 22:51)

Even in the Garden of Gethsemane, as Jesus faced his cruel passion and dreadful death, he was more concerned about others than about himself. "He touched the servant's ear and healed him."

The servant came to arrest Jesus and take him prisoner, but that did not deter Jesus from extending his healing love to him. Jesus' love always reaches out to everyone, even to his enemies.

With such an example of love, should we not strive to imitate his love by being lovingly concerned about others, even to those who might not appeal to us?

20 *He himself bore our sins in his body upon the cross, so that, free from sin, we might live for righteousness. By his wounds you have been healed.* (1 Pt 2:24)

Could there be any greater healing than being absolved of all our sinfulness? By redeeming us, Jesus restored our fragmented relationship with the Father and also gave us the potential of receiving his divine life and love.

Gazing at your crucifix, listen to Jesus say: "No one has greater love than this, to lay down one's life for one's friends" (Jn 15:13).

HOLY SPIRIT

21 ... *"Do not be afraid, Mary, ... The holy Spirit will come upon you, and the power of the Most High will overshadow you. ..."*

(Lk 1:30, 35)

Throughout Scripture, whenever the presence or power of God is evident, we hear those reassuring words: "Do not be afraid." When Mary was asked to become the Mother of the Messiah in such an unusual way without a natural father, she, too, was anxious and uncertain. The Holy Spirit came upon her to relieve all her fears and doubts.

When the Lord asks us to undertake a certain duty or responsibility, the healing love of the Holy Spirit will clear away many of our fears and misgivings.

> The LORD is my life's refuge;
> of whom shall I be afraid? (Ps 27:1)

22 ... *Elizabeth, filled with the holy Spirit, cried out in a loud voice and said, "Most blessed are you among women, and blessed is the fruit of your womb. And how does this happen to me, that the mother of my Lord should come to me?"* (Lk 1:41-43)

Elizabeth was persecuted all her life because of her infertility, which in her day was considered a punishment from God.

She could have been envious of Mary, thus creating a strained relationship between herself and her young kinswoman who was pregnant with the Messiah.

However, Elizabeth was filled with the Holy Spirit, who had healed her of any such human reactions or tendencies. Come Holy Spirit with your healing power.

23 *". . . He will baptize you with the holy Spirit and fire."* (Mt 3:11)

We are accustomed to call the Holy Spirit the fire of divine love, because of the intensity of his love which we received in our baptism. Fire is a purifying process whereby dross is extracted from precious metal.

Since "our God is a consuming fire" (Heb 12:29), he heals us by burning away our pride, self-centeredness, and all the other undesirable weaknesses which impede our progress on the road to holiness.

O Holy Spirit, make us always receptive to the purifying fire of your divine love.

24 *"I have much more to tell you, but you cannot bear it now. But when he comes, the Spirit of truth, he will guide you to all truth. . . ."* (Jn 16:12-13)

Jesus sent the Holy Spirit upon us to help us meet all the demands of daily living. We may be perplexed or wonder what the Lord is asking of us in a given situation. What is the Lord's will for me? Which avenue should I choose?

The Holy Spirit comes to our rescue in these mini-crises. His gifts of wisdom and knowledge help us clear away our doubts and indecisions. He constantly enlightens and guides us to all truth, as Jesus promised. The psalmist gives us reassurance when he reminds us:

> The LORD is my light and my salvation;
> whom should I fear? . . . (Ps 27:1)

25 *. . . "Saul, my brother, the Lord has sent me, Jesus who appeared to you on the way by which you came, that you may regain your sight and be filled with the holy Spirit."* (Acts 9:17)

As Paul was filled with the Holy Spirit, he was healed of a twofold blindness. His blindness was physical as well as spiritual. The healing power of the Spirit transformed him from an avowed persecutor to a dedicated disciple of the Lord.

The presence and power of the Holy Spirit in our lives will help us by endowing us with a gift of discernment, enabling us to see more clearly God's plan in our lives.

Come, Holy Spirit, with your healing power.

26 *... The holy Spirit also testifies to us, ... he also says: / "Their sins and their evildoing / I will remember no more."* (Heb 10:15, 17)

We praise and thank the Holy Spirit as our Sanctifier. The first step he takes in the process of purifying us is to forgive our sinfulness.

Jesus pointed out this special work of the Holy Spirit when he empowered the apostles to forgive sins. Note that he first imparted to them the Holy Spirit. "He breathed on them and said to them, 'Receive the holy Spirit. Whose sins you forgive are forgiven ...' " (Jn 20:22).

Thank you, Holy Spirit, for forgiving me so very many times when I failed you.

27 *To each individual the manifestation of the Spirit is given for some benefit. . . . to another gifts of healing by the one Spirit.*
(1 Cor 12:7, 9)

The Holy Spirit can and does heal directly or through the sacramental rites of the church. He may wish to heal through some person or even through ourselves. We should never hesitate to pray with and for others that the Lord might heal them.

Remembering that the gifts of the Spirit are always given for the benefit of the community should remove any fear that may deter us from praying for a healing for ourselves or for another person.

Through the power of your divine love, O Holy Spirit, heal us of all that needs healing.

28 *Do not quench the Spirit.* (1 Thes 5:19)

The healing power of the Holy Spirit operates dynamically within us, helping us to remove any obstacle or hindrance that may prevent us from becoming the kind of people he wants us to be.

We can quench the Holy Spirit by not listening to the inspirations he gives us, by neglecting to spend time in prayer, especially the prayer of listening, or by not being receptive to the love he wishes to pour into our hearts.

Heal me, O Spirit of God, in spite of my reluctance to give myself totally to you.

29 *For God did not give us a spirit of cowardice but rather of power and love and self-control.* (2 Tm 1:7)

When the Holy Spirit invites us to follow the Christian way of life laid down by Jesus, he knows that it will take courage to dare to be different from the world. He abides with us to heal us of any fear, hesitation, or cowardice which may plague us.

The Spirit empowers us to say yes to the Lord even though it may not be the popular mode of conduct. He continues to fill us with his love, which is the motivating power enabling us to take up our cross daily and follow the Lord.

Help us, Holy Spirit, in our weak moments.

30 *"The Advocate, the holy Spirit that the Father will send in my name—he will teach you everything and remind you of all that [I] told you."* (Jn 14:26)

Jesus promised that the Advocate whom the Father would send in his name would remain to inspire and guide us through the many problem areas which arise on our pilgrim journey. His healing love will remove all the worries and anxieties which torment us in making a decision.

The Holy Spirit will enlighten us and teach us how the Gospel truths taught by Jesus apply in our daily living.

Come, Holy Spirit, enlighten our minds and hearts.

HOLY TRINITY

31 *The spirit of the Lord GOD is upon me, / because the LORD has anointed me; / He has sent me to bring glad tidings to the lowly, / to heal the brokenhearted, / To proclaim liberty to the captives / and release to the prisoners.* (Is 61:1)

This prophecy, proclaimed eight hundred years before the Incarnation, reveals the involvement of all three persons of the Blessed Trinity in our redemption and sanctification. The Father sent Jesus as our Redeemer, the Spirit anointed him for his mission on earth. These meticulous plans of God, announced centuries before, prove the Lord's unbounded love for us.

Glory be to the Father, and to the Son, and to the Holy Spirit! Amen.

Faith, a Divine Gift

. . . Faith comes from what is heard, and what is heard comes through the word of Christ. (Rom 10:17)

FATHER

1 *"Do not let your hearts be troubled. You have faith in God; have faith also in me."* (Jn 14:1)

Scripture defines faith in these words: "Faith is the realization of what is hoped for and evidence of things not seen" (Heb 11:1).

The first level of faith, intellectual faith, helps us believe a truth we cannot understand, but can accept on the evidence of revelation.

The next level is the faith of commitment. We believe so firmly in a program, project, or way of life that we are willing to contribute our time, energy, and talent to pursue it.

The third level is the faith of expectancy. We simply know and trust that God will act in every given situation. Mary is a perfect model of this degree of faith.

With the apostles we pray: "Lord, increase our faith" (Lk 17:5).

2 *Abram put his faith in the LORD, who credited it to him as an act of righteousness.*

(Gn 15:6)

Abram is rightly called the father of faith. He believed that the call he heard did really come from God, even though the belief in one true God was almost unknown at the time. Abram responded to that call by leaving home and his native country to relocate in a land the Lord pointed out to him. Such a response required great faith and confidence in God.

Even a brief reflection on Abram's faith will be a great support to us when the Lord calls us to undertake some seemingly difficult task or to assume some grave burden.

Our faith response will greatly please the Lord.

3 *Was not Abraham our father justified by works when he offered his son Isaac upon the altar? You see that faith was active along with his works, and faith was completed by the works.*

(Jas 2:21-22)

Abraham's faith was not a passive "I believe" to the Lord, but it was a faith of commitment. This kind of faith is willing to contribute time, talent, and treasure to a good work.

A committed faith, like Abraham's, sometimes faces paradoxes. God had promised that Abraham's progeny would be as numerous as the grains of sand on the shore, yet the same God now asked Abraham to sacrifice his son Isaac, his only hope for descendants. Yet Abraham's strong vibrant faith prevailed, and God fulfilled his promise.

Father, may our faith face every paradox and withstand every test you are pleased to send.

4 *By faith Abel offered to God a sacrifice greater than Cain's. Through this he was attested to be righteous, God bearing witness to his gifts, and through this, though dead, he still speaks.*

(Heb 11:4)

The Lord was pleased with Abel's offering of himself symbolized by the gift of the firstlings of his flock. Abel offered these with reverence and devotion, with humility and thanksgiving. His example speaks eloquently to us today.

We are privileged to make the gift of ourselves to the Lord in every celebration of the Eucharist. We are aptly represented by the gifts of bread and wine which are essential for sustaining life. The Lord looks beyond the externals to the dispositions of our heart. This is our offering in "spirit and truth."

Lord, may our sacrifice always be pleasing to you.

5 *By faith Noah, warned about what was not yet seen, with reverence built an ark for the salvation of his household. . . .* (Heb 11:7)

Noah placed his faith in the words of the Lord that a flood would come to destroy the world. He persevered in his faith until he had built the ark. It was Noah's faith which brought "salvation to his household."

By a process that resembles osmosis, the fervent faith of parents is passed on to their children. Parents' trust and confidence in God will be engendered in their family as a precious inheritance.

Thank you, Lord, for the faith of our parents.

6 *. . . Without faith it is impossible to please him, for anyone who approaches God must believe that he exists and that he rewards those who seek him.* (Heb 11:6)

In our age of transition we are experiencing a widespread crisis in faith. The vast advances in knowledge and technology have made us a proud, sophisticated people who do not feel any need for God in our lives.

Jesus had the same experience with the so-called learned of his day. He praised his Father for the childlike faith of the humble people who believed in him.

Realizing that it is impossible to please God without faith, may our prayer be the same as the father of the possessed boy: "I do believe, help my unbelief!" (Mk 9:24).

7 *No one who waits for you shall be put to shame; / those shall be put to shame who heedlessly break faith.* (Ps 25:3)

The psalmist reminds us that our God is a faithful God. Throughout the whole history of salvation, he has always kept his promises. God's fidelity is the fruit of his boundless, unconditional love for each one of us personally. He provides for us, protects us, forgives us, and cares for us every moment of the day.

The principal response the Lord wants from us is our love and gratefulness. As our love for him increases, we will be able to place more and more trust and confidence in him, regardless of what he may ask of us.

Lord, help me to "wait on you" by fulfilling your will all the days of my life.

8 *Have we not all the one Father? / Has not the one God created us? / Why then do we break faith with each other, / violating the covenant of our fathers?* (Mal 2:10)

Every time we pray "Our Father," we acknowledge that God is our common Father. Our faith assures us that we belong to the family of God and are brothers and sisters to one another.

Nonetheless, our faith is a maturing faith, and we may experience lapses when we are unjustly accused, criticized, or ridiculed. We are apt to strike back at the attack, oblivious for the moment that we are all members of the body of Christ and that Jesus told us to love our neighbor as ourselves.

These lapses can help our faith mature if we humbly acknowledge our failure and beg the Father's forgiveness.

9 *For upright is the word of the LORD, / and all his works are trustworthy.* (Ps 33:4)

As we pray with the Word of God, we learn to know the Lord as a loving, gracious Father who is always faithful to that word. We find that he can always be trusted in all the circumstances of our life.

Time has taught us that when we have

experienced something seemingly tragic, the passage of time has often proved it to be a great boon and blessing. When this occurs, we can almost see the Lord smiling and saying: "trust me."

May we never give him cause to say to us as he did to his disciples: "Why are you terrified, O you of little faith?" (Mt 8:26).

10 *God added his testimony by signs, wonders, various acts of power, and distribution of the gifts of the holy Spirit according to his will.* (Heb 2:4)

Our patient Father knows how weak our faith is at times and how often we may doubt him. He also understands how difficult it may be for us to trust him unconditionally. For this reason he has demonstrated his divine power and loving concern by all kinds of signs and wonders.

He also gave the gifts of his Spirit so that our faith would be strengthened and we would have the courage and submission to accept willingly whatever the Father asks of us.

Great is our Lord and mighty in power;
to his wisdom there is no limit. (Ps 147:5)

SON

11 ... *"Where is the newborn king of the Jews? We saw his star at its rising and have come to do him homage."* (Mt 2:2)

The Wise Men made a difficult and dangerous journey to pay homage to Jesus, the newborn King of the Jews. They were convinced and motivated by a strong faith based on some flimsy evidence: "We saw his star at its rising."

Their persevering faith never wavered throughout the arduous journey. That their faith enabled them to recognize Jesus as a priest, king, and redeemer is attested by the nature of their gifts of gold, frankincense, and myrrh.

Jesus, with your grace, may our weak faith mature into a strong faith of expectancy.

12 *The Lord replied. "If you have faith the size of a mustard seed, you would say to [this] mulberry tree, 'Be uprooted and planted in the sea,' and it would obey you."* (Lk 17:6)

Faith is a powerful force in the world and in our own lives. We may think of ourselves as tiny mustard seed, too unimportant to accept a certain position, or too incapable to undertake a particular task. However, if we do so with faith and trust in the Lord, we will be able to accomplish much more than we ever thought possible.

Someone said: "With faith we can do the hard things immediately, but it takes a little longer to do the impossible."

Lord, help me to acknowledge my own inadequacy and, with greater confidence and trust, rely on your grace and help.

13 *When he saw their faith, he said, "As for you, your sins are forgiven."* (Lk 5:20)

Jesus was deeply pleased with the faith of those men who overcame many difficulties to bring the paralytic before him to ask for a healing. As usual, Jesus healed the whole person. He did not only heal the man physically, but he forgave him his sins.

When we come before the Lord with a strong expectant faith, we can be certain that Jesus will respond to our prayer far beyond our expectations.

May our faith enable us to bring others to you.

14 *"Whatever you ask for in prayer with faith, you will receive."* (Mt 21:22)

Jesus did not promise that every specific thing we ask for in prayer would be granted, but rather that our prayer with faith would bear fruit. Prayer is a conditioning process for us. We pray primarily that our will and attitude, our heart and mind, may be in tune with God's will for us.

It requires faith and trust in God to pray with this spirit of resignation. Prayer is our relationship with our God, and the deeper our relationship becomes, the more easily will we conform to his plan for us.

Lord, teach us to pray with this committed faith.

15 *Jesus answered and said to them, "This is the work of God, that you believe in the one he sent." (Jn 6:29)*

Jesus was always pleased when people believed in him. He was eager to have them recognize him as the Redeemer sent into the world and to believe his teachings, even though they were radically different from what they had learned. When people believed in him, Jesus worked many miracles to prove the authenticity of his teaching.

On the other hand, Jesus was deeply disappointed when the proud and so-called learned refused to accept or believe in him. At Nazareth "he did not work many mighty deeds there because of their lack of faith" (Mt 13:58).

May our hearts be filled with a fervent faith so that the Lord might work many wonders in us and through us!

16 *". . . Even if you do not believe me, believe the works, so that you may realize [and understand] that the Father is in me and I am in the Father."* (Jn 10:38)

Jesus manifested infinite patience with those who would not believe in him. He endeavored to open their minds and hearts by appealing to the works he was doing, which obviously required divine power to perform.

He also identified himself with the Father and assured them that the Father and he were one. Thus he proclaimed his divinity, but to no avail. It did not touch or change the hearts of those who opposed him.

Thank you, Lord, for the gift of faith. May it flourish more brilliantly in all we do.

17 *When Jesus heard this, he was amazed and said to those following him, "Amen, I say to you, in no one in Israel have I found such faith."* (Mt 8:10)

Jesus was delighted with the faith of the military officer who begged him to heal his servant. Servants could be bought and sold very easily at that time, but the centurion had a special place in his heart for this particular servant, which motivated him to overcome his pride and seek out Jesus to ask for the healing.

Jesus' pleasure encourages us to exercise

our faith in him that it may grow and mature within us. Like the centurion, our faith must be expressed with loving concern for others.

The humble attitude of the centurion is heard in every Mass: "Lord, I am not worthy to have you enter under my roof."

18 . . . *"I am the resurrection and the life; whoever believes in me, even if he dies, will live, and everyone who lives and believes in me will never die. Do you believe this?"* (Jn 11:25-26)

The resurrection of Jesus from the dead puts the seal of truth on everything he taught. Our faith assures us that just as Jesus rose, so we will also rise with him on the day he calls us to our heavenly home. Jesus proclaims this truth many times and always punctuates it with: "Do you believe this?"

The resurrection of Jesus was the constant teaching of St. Paul: "Just as Christ was raised from the dead by the glory of the Father, we too might live in newness of life" (Rom 6:4).

We need to permit this faith-conviction to grow by joining Martha as she says, "Yes, Lord, I do believe."

19 *". . . I have prayed that your own faith may not fail; and once you have turned back, you must strengthen your brothers."* (Lk 22:32)

Peter did not recognize his own weakness and lack of faith. Jesus foresaw his fall and prayed that he would arise with a stronger, more committed faith. History proved that Jesus' prayer was answered, for Peter became a pillar of faith and an example to all his brothers.

When we acknowledge our own weak faith and pray fervently with Jesus for a stronger, more dynamic faith, we can be certain he will be there to assist us when our faith is tested.

May our prayer always be: "Lord, increase our faith."

20 *And he said to them, "Oh, how foolish you are! How slow of heart to believe all that the prophets spoke!"* (Lk 24:25)

On their journey to Emmaus, the two disciples were completely shattered at the death of Jesus. All their hopes for a Messiah who would deliver them from the power of Rome evaporated into thin air. Jesus chided them and patiently led them into an understanding of what Scripture had revealed about the Messiah.

As we journey down the roadway of life,

we will experience occasions when we may be disappointed and even discouraged about the turn of events. Momentarily we forget that God's ways are not our ways. We may temporarily be oblivious that Jesus is walking with us because "our eyes are prevented from recognizing him."

Jesus reminds us: "Behold, I am with you always" (Mt 28:20).

HOLY SPIRIT

21 *"To each individual the manifestation of the Spirit is given for some benefit . . . to another faith by the same Spirit. . . ."* (1 Cor 12:7, 9)

The Holy Spirit endows each one of us individually with his spiritual gifts. These gifts are indispensable if we are to safely complete our journey heavenward. However, they are not given to be used exclusively for ourselves. We are to use them to draw others closer to the Lord and to assist them as they journey through life.

As we radiate our own confidence and trust in the Lord, it will touch others. If peace and joy fill our hearts, they will also be reflected in all we do. Our lifestyle makes others receptive to the Lord's gifts.

Holy Spirit, as you are so generous in

giving your gifts to us, may we graciously and generously share with others.

22 *That he may grant you in accord with the riches of his glory to be strengthened with power through his Spirit in the inner self.*

(Eph 3:16)

These words are only a brief excerpt from Paul's fervent prayer for our growth and progress on our spiritual journey. We cannot reach total spiritual maturity in this life, but our striving each day will bring us one step closer in our relationship with the Lord.

Life consists of going from one conversion to another. However, each conversion is a growth process filling us with the fullness of God. This is the work of the Holy Spirit dwelling within us. He inspires, guides, encourages, and strengthens us as we plod along life's highway.

May his abiding presence keep us ever going forward.

23 *. . . We have the same spirit of faith, according to what is written, "I believed, therefore I spoke," we too believe and therefore speak.*

(2 Cor 4:13)

With the divine gift of faith from the Holy Spirit we are able to believe all that was revealed. The gifts of the Spirit are given for a twofold purpose: for our own personal sanctification and also for the common good in building up the body of Christ.

We do use these gifts when we speak kindly and gently without bitterness or criticism. Our firm faith and trust in the Lord is reflected in all our words and actions. Our lifestyle is also a way of speaking.

May we always give witness to the faith that has been given us.

24 *He [Barnabas] was a good man, filled with the holy Spirit and faith. And a large number of people was added to the Lord.*

(Acts 11:24)

Barnabas received a special call to become a disciple and also to proclaim the good news to the Gentiles. In responding to that call, he was open to the influence of the Holy Spirit, who filled him with divine gifts. His radiant faith and his exceptional goodness were apparent to all who met him. Thus the Holy Spirit prepared him for his ministry.

We are also called as disciples to a personal ministry. The Holy Spirit, who we received at baptism, continues to equip us for our ministry. He strengthens our faith and fills us with his love so that we may more easily accept and love others.

"... The love of God has been poured out into our hearts through the holy Spirit that has been given to us" (Rom 5:5).

Faith, a Divine Gift / 177

25 *". . . God, who knows the heart, bore witness by granting them the holy Spirit just as he did us."* (Acts 15:8)

In this very first Council in the church, St. Peter gave witness to the faith of the early converts. He rightly attributed the conversion of the Gentiles to the outpouring of the Holy Spirit upon them with a gift of faith.

Our faith assures us that the Holy Spirit is guiding and directing the church in this age of transition. We may have some concerns about the conditions in the church today, but our faith will remind us that the Lord promised his church would prevail, "and the gates of the netherworld shall not prevail against it" (Mt 16:18).

Holy Spirit, enkindle in the hearts of all Christians a committed, persevering faith.

26 *. . . My message and my proclamation were not with persuasive [words of] wisdom, but with a demonstration of spirit and power, so that your faith might rest not on human wisdom but on the power of God.* (1 Cor 2:4-5)

Throughout his apostolate to the Gentiles, St. Paul was inspired and empowered by the Holy Spirit to an eminent degree. Guided by the Spirit, Paul was able to bring countless souls into the fold of Christ.

That same Holy Spirit, dwelling with us, enlightens and inspires us as we strive to fulfill our mission in life. He also shares his divine power with us, enabling us to accomplish many tasks which of ourselves we could never succeed in doing.

Spirit of God, give us an attentive heart and a willingness to forget self and rely on your Spirit, that your will might be accomplished through us.

27 *In all circumstances, hold faith as a shield, to quench all [the] flaming arrows of the evil one. And take the helmet of salvation and the sword of the Spirit, which is the word of God.*

(Eph 6:16, 17)

Our life on earth is a warfare, a struggle between the clamoring forces of evil and the gentle persuasion of the Holy Spirit to walk in his light. The military parlance used in Scripture indicates how difficult the battle may become.

In all circumstances we have at hand "the sword of the Spirit, which is the word of God." In that Word, Jesus gives us an example by his own struggle with the devil in the desert. The Holy Spirit assures us: "My grace is sufficient for you, for power is made perfect in weakness" (2 Cor 12:9).

At all times we have the assurance of the Spirit's loving protection.

28 *For by grace you have been saved through faith, and this is not from you; it is the gift of God.* (Eph 2:8)

When Jesus completed his redemptive work on earth, he sent the Holy Spirit to carry on the work of our sanctification. The Spirit begins his work by planting the seed of faith in our hearts, then grants grace to cause it to grow and mature, like the mustard seed growing into a large bush.

As our faith becomes stronger, we become more receptive to the working of the Spirit within us that conditions us for his final gift of salvation. We cannot earn or merit this gift of salvation. We can only be docile to the Holy Spirit and permit him to transform us into a fit candidate for heaven.

"I do believe, help my unbelief!" (Mk 9:24).

29 *Now the one who has prepared us for this very thing is God, who has given us the Spirit as a first installment.* (2 Cor 5:5)

God graciously prepared us for our eternal destiny by sending his Son, Jesus, into our sinful world to redeem us. When he had finished his ministry, he sent the Holy Spirit to fill us with his divine life and love as the "first installment" of our heavenly inheritance.

The Holy Spirit purifies and sanctifies us as we journey through life. He helps us recognize the malice of sin and creates within us a longing for all that is good and holy. He gives us discernment, motivation, and strength to pursue the way of life which Jesus has mapped out for us.

What a comforting privilege to be a member in faith of the family of God.

30 *For through the Spirit, by faith, we await the hope of righteousness.* (Gal 5:5)

Faith is one of the precious gifts of the Holy Spirit. As we joyfully receive this gift and eagerly cooperate with the grace of the Holy Spirit, our faith will reach the level of expectancy where we simply know that God will take care of every situation in our lives.

With this level of faith, we look with confidence and trust in the Lord, beyond the bounds of our earthly life to that state:

> "What eye has not seen, and ear has not heard,
> and what has not entered the human heart,
> what God has prepared for those who love him." (1 Cor 2:9)

Lord, enkindle my faith that I may eagerly look forward to that life of eternal peace and joy with you forever!

HOLY TRINITY

31 *For this reason I kneel before the Father, from whom every family in heaven and on earth is named, that he may grant you in accord with the riches of his glory to be strengthened with power through his Spirit in the inner self, and that Christ may dwell in your heart through faith; that you, rooted and grounded in love, may have strength to comprehend with all the holy ones what is the breadth and length and height and depth, and to know the love of Christ that surpasses knowledge, so that you may be filled with all the fullness of God.* (Eph 3:14-19)

This prayer of petition is pleasing to the Lord, since it is addressed to all three persons of the Blessed Trinity in acknowledgment of their specific roles in the work of our salvation.

Make this powerful prayer addressed to the Holy Trinity your own, by changing the second person pronoun to the first person.

If you wish to pray for another person, you may eliminate the same pronoun and insert the name of the person for whom you are praying.

Making this scriptural passage addressed to the Holy Trinity a daily prayer will greatly enrich your faith and bring much peace.

Hope Enriches Expectation

. . . We await the blessed hope, the appearance of the glory of the great God and of our savior Jesus Christ. (Ti 2:13)

FATHER

1 *For in him our hearts rejoice; / in his holy name we trust. / May your kindness, O LORD, be upon us / who have put our hope in you.*
(Ps 33:21-22)

The virtue of hope creates within us an expectation that the kindness of our loving Father will envelop us at all times and that his protective arm be ever around us. We know he will never abandon us. This reassurance causes our hearts to rejoice at the goodness of the Lord.

Lord, I place all my hope and trust in you. May your ever-present kindness continue to fill my heart with an even greater hope of expectancy.

2 *Trust God and he will help you; make straight your ways and hope in him.* (Sir 2:6)

God knows how inadequate we are to cling to the truth with all the illusions of life taking place around us. We long for new strength in our hopes and dreams. Even as we remember how infinitely good God is, we need to turn to him yet more hopefully and trust him more fully.

We make our ways straight by striving to see God's will and his divine plan in all that occurs in life, even though we may not understand the pain and disappointment that may accompany it.

Keep forever reminding us, Lord, to keep on keeping on: hoping, striving, trusting. May we find real joy in putting all our hope in you.

3 *Take courage and be stouthearted, / all you who hope in the LORD.* (Ps 31:25)

When we are convinced of God's unconditional love for us, we will be eternally optimistic. Our optimism gives us the assurance that our ever-vigilant Father is watching over us at all times. The Father is pleased that our hope gives us the courage to place all our trust and expectations in him.

Keep us brave and stouthearted, Father, as we launch out into the deep currents of everyday life, and may our expectant hope

bring us the comfort, peace, and joy which
you desire for us.

> They that hope in the LORD will renew
>   their strength,
>   they will soar as with eagles' wings;
> They will run and not grow weary,
>   walk and not grow faint. (Is 40:31)

4 *Lively is the courage of those who fear the
LORD, for they put their hope in their savior.*
(Sir 34:13)

Fear of the Lord is a deep reverence,
wonder, and awe at the extravagance of the
Lord's limitless love for us. It gives us the
courage to throw unwarranted caution to
the wind when the Lord prompts us to
respond to his inspirations in our daily
ministry.

Lord, continue your gracious benevolence
to us, that our confidence may be so fortified
that it will enkindle greater hope and expectation in all those who come our way. Keep
our own hope lively and our courage daring.

5 *May your kindness, O LORD, be upon us who
have put our hope in you.* (Ps 33:22)

Human kindness may be only an occasional experience. The Lord knows that
kindness may not be shown us when we
need it, that is why he reminds us that his

kindness is always "upon us who have put our hope in you."

Our awareness of the Father's ever-present kindness should remove any fear or anxiety from our hearts. His constant, unwavering affection should motivate us to extend our kindness to others more generously.

Father, as your kindness daily overshadows us, may our gratitude become more intense, and may our hope and trust grow ever stronger.

6 *You shall return by the help of your God, / if you remain loyal and do right / and always hope in your God.* (Hos 12:7)

Our sinfulness leads us away from the Lord and leaves only the ashes of disillusionment. The peace we once enjoyed ebbs away as a cloud of gloom and depression descends upon us. The clever enticements of the evil one will eventually lead us down the road to despair.

Fortunately, our Father is a God of infinite mercy and compassion. If we turn to him, he will rekindle our hope. This hope inspires and motivates us to "remain loyal and do right."

Hope leads us back to our merciful Father, and peace and joy will dissipate the clouds of gloom and discouragement. Father, we hope in you always.

7 *Why are you so downcast, O my soul? / Why do you sigh within me? / Hope in God! For I shall again be thanking him, / in the presence of my savior and my God.* (Ps 42:12)

What an encouraging soliloquy! How fruitful this self-examination! How groundless and depressing our fears can be! A reflection on the unconditional, enduring love of God will quicken our hope.

As we pause to thank and praise the Lord for his creating, caring, forgiving, healing, redeeming love which overshadows us at every turn of the road, our faith, hope, and love for our gracious Father will grow. We will be filled with that peace the world cannot give.

Lord, help me to put all my hope and trust in you and your divine plan in my life.

8 *. . . I will look to the LORD, / I will put my trust in God my savior; / my God will hear me.* (Mi 7:7)

God is all things, he is in all things, he has all things in his command. He is most eager and ready to give us whatever we need if we ask him with trust and confidence. Our asking him is often imperfect and lacks that childlike trust which is so pleasing to our faithful Father.

Father, daily, hourly, moment by moment, your gracious goodness cares for us. Yet we easily become overly anxious or unduly concerned when our pathway becomes steep, rocky, and rough.

Fill us with that hope in your goodness that we may keep our focus ever riveted on you.

9 *Most admirable and worthy of everlasting remembrance was the mother, who saw her seven sons perish in a single day, yet bore it courageously because of her hope in the LORD.*

(2 Mc 7:20)

The mother of the seven sons who were martyred was the embodiment of the theological virtues of faith, hope, and love. Her vibrant faith in God and in the life hereafter intensified her great love for God which, in turn, generated her hope in his promise of everlasting glory. In spite of the anguish of seeing her seven sons perish, she was at peace thanks to her fervent hope.

As Mary stood beneath the cross of her Son, she too, manifested her dynamic faith, her intense love, and her fervent love in the redemption of the human race.

Mother of faith, hope, and love, pray for us.

10 *Blessed be the God and Father of our Lord Jesus Christ, the Father of compassion and God of all encouragement, who encourages us in our every affliction. . . .* (2 Cor 1:3-4)

How precious are those times in our life which challenge our trust and confidence in our God of compassion. A death of a loved one may be such an occasion. Rising above the pain of loss and separation is the realization of the love, peace, and eternal bliss of heaven which our loved one is enjoying.

Our God of compassion accompanies us through every affliction, bringing us comfort and consolation.

What a blessing is the Spirit's gift of hope! What confidence and trust it inspires!

SON

11 *"Behold my servant whom I have chosen, / my beloved in whom I delight . . . / And in his name the Gentiles will hope."* (Mt 12:18, 21)

Centuries before Jesus came into our world, the Father through his prophet Isaiah gave us much reason to place all our hope in his goodness. The Father not only promised his Son as our Redeemer, but called us Gentiles through the gift of faith to become members of his family and heirs to his kingdom.

Listen to John's moving words: "For God so loved the world that he gave his only Son, so that everyone who believes in him might not perish but might have eternal life" (Jn 3:16).

Do we need further reason to enkindle a greater hope, confidence, and trust in our loving Father?

12 *At once [Jesus] spoke to them, "Take courage, it is I; do not be afraid."* (Mt 14:27)

Jesus is speaking to us as surely as to Peter when he bids us to take a risk, to hold on when the winds and waves of adversity threaten to inundate us. Jesus is faithful to his promise to be with us always and everywhere. We must reach out to him, cling to him. Knowing his love and fidelity spurs us to greater heights of hope and expectancy.

Lord Jesus, you know how often we turn to those who really cannot help us. Too often we turn to you only when others fail. Transform our hearts and minds to place greater hope, confidence, and trust in you. We know that you are pleased when we do so.

13 ... *"Lord, have pity on my son."* ... *Jesus rebuked him and the demon came out of him, and from that hour the boy was cured.*

(Mt 17:15, 18)

The possessed boy's father was desperate. He wanted his son freed from the power of the evil spirit. He saw Jesus as his only and last hope, since the disciples had failed to expel the demon. When the disciples asked Jesus why they could not cast out the devil Jesus said plainly: "Because of your little faith."

When life becomes perplexing, anxiety-ridden, and painful, we, too, become desperate. Even though our gift of hope should help us meet every contingency, it seems to fade at such critical times. However, the Lord meets us where we are as he did in the Gospel account. His presence and power come to our rescue.

Lord, grace us with a fervent hope, especially in trying moments.

14 *"Do not be afraid any longer, little flock, for your Father is pleased to give you the kingdom."* (Lk 12:32)

Jesus is spurring us on to greater hope. He is encouraging us to detach ourselves from material things and place all our hope in the promise of eternal life which the Father wants to give us.

The more detached we are from material things and from the cares and concerns of this life, the more easily will we be able to concentrate on our eternal destiny. A question which should come to mind frequently as we make decisions is: "What value has this for eternity?" Such a question will not only keep our hope alive, but will enkindle it so brightly that it becomes the guiding light on our journey back to our Father.

Father, thank you for the kingdom which you so graciously promised us. Thank you for calling us to be members of your "little flock."

15 *In him we were also chosen . . . so that we might exist for the praise of his glory, we who first hoped in Christ.* (Eph 1:11-12)

Jesus taught us by word and example how to place all our hope in our loving Father. As adopted children of our heavenly Father, we should have no fear or anxiety, since we are living under the watchful eyes of our gracious God whose enduring love envelops us always and everywhere.

This conviction not only generates great hope within us, but it also makes our hearts vibrate with praise, honor, and glory for such a wonderful God. Jesus set the example for us as he paused to raise his prayer of praise and thanksgiving heavenward. "I give praise to you, Father, Lord of heaven and earth, for although you have hidden these things from the wise and the learned you have revealed them to the childlike" (Mt 11:25).

16 *"Lord, if you had been here, my brother would not have died...." Jesus said to her, "Your brother will rise." Martha said to him, "I know he will rise, in the resurrection on the last day."* (Jn 11:21, 23-24)

Martha loved Jesus and trusted in his words, even though resurrection from the dead was not universally believed at that time. It was her firm hope that convinced her that her brother, Lazarus, would rise again.

Jesus instills great hope in us when he assures us: "I am the resurrection and the life." This truth gives meaning and purpose to life here on earth. Our life on earth is a conditioning, a preparation for life hereafter. Little wonder that the Easter liturgy bids us sing joyously the Alleluias of praise and glory.

17 *May our Lord Jesus Christ himself and God our Father, who has loved us and given us everlasting encouragement and good hope through his grace, encourage your hearts and strengthen them in every good deed and word.*

(2 Thes 2:16-17)

It is impossible to live without hope. Hope helps us see the smile of God as we live in his presence and find that constant source of inner strength. He encourages us in all our undertakings.

Help us, Lord, to keep our eyes fixed on you. Help us place "every good deed and word" in your hands where we will find meaning and comfort.

May our radiant hope enliven the hope in the hearts of all those who are in dire need of your encouragement.

18 *Rejoice in hope, endure in affliction, persevere in prayer.* (Rom 12:12)

Rejoice in hope: hope always looks to the future with an expectant, happy outcome. As Christians we look forward with hope to the eternal peace and joy of our heavenly home. This gives us reason to rejoice in hope.

Endure affliction: given our human condition, afflictions are part of the fabric of life. By enduring afflictions, Jesus sanctified all sufferings and inconveniences and made them redemptive.

Persevere in prayer: prayer is our relationship with God, expressed in countless ways. The more time we spend in prayer and the more fervent our prayer, the more intimate will be our relationship with our loving Lord.

Lord, you have given us so many reasons to rejoice in hope.

19 *For we have heard of your faith in Christ Jesus and the love that you have for all the holy ones because of the hope reserved for you in heaven. . . .* (Col 1:4-5)

Hope is optimism at its best. Our anticipation of a happy outcome for all the troubles of the day is evidence of the forebearance and strength which hope creates within us. Our ability to depend on the Lord and hope in his promises sustains us and engenders peace in our hearts.

Lord, we are not as upbeat as we ought to be at times, but help us to anticipate your extravagant promises to us. Help us to be resurrection people who always look redeemed.

20 *And we have this confidence in him, that if we ask anything according to his will, he hears us.* (1 Jn 5:14)

As we proceed on our pilgrimage through life, essential dispositions are hope, confidence, and trust. With these we may persevere onward to our eternal destiny. We also need divine assistance for every step of the journey.

Since our Father longs for us to reach our home with him, he generously and gladly provides us with every grace and gift we need along the way. When we humbly and sincerely acknowledge our dependence on him and ask for what is essential for our pilgrimage heavenward, we can be certain that we are asking "according to his will."

This is all contained in that familiar petition we make each day: "Give us this day our daily bread." Thank you, Lord, for responding so graciously to our request.

HOLY SPIRIT

21 *May the eyes of [your] hearts be enlightened, that you may know what is the hope that belongs to his call, what are the riches of glory in his inheritance among the holy ones.* (Eph 1:18)

Our eyes see only a few steps down the road and our hearts, too, can only grasp a limited dimension of God's goodness. As the Holy Spirit enlightens the eyes of our hearts, our vision becomes more cosmic and our hope soars.

The Lord has called us to the riches of glory and to an everlasting inheritance with all the saints in heaven. Doubt, fear, and an unworthiness syndrome curtail our joy in striving for that end. The Holy Spirit's gift of hope comes to our rescue with the assurance of God's love for us and his eagerness to give us all the help we need as we journey forth.

Holy Spirit, continue to change our focus and increase the hope in our hearts.

22 *That he may grant you in accord with the riches of his glory to be strengthened with power through his Spirit in the inner self, and that Christ may dwell in your hearts through faith; that you, [may be] rooted and grounded in love.*

(Eph 3:16-17)

Since we all belong to the communion of saints, we are a privileged people. We are all adopted children of our Father. As members of the family of God, we support one another with our love and our prayers. St. Paul prays earnestly for us that the Trinitarian life may flourish in us.

When we became the temple of the Holy Spirit, the whole Trinity came to dwell within us. Through the dynamic presence of

198 / *Know Me*

the three Divine Persons, our faith is increased and we are "rooted and grounded in love," thus enkindling a more vibrant hope, trust, reassurance, and confidence in all the promises the Lord has made to us.

Come, Holy Spirit, strengthen our faith, hope, and love.

23 *Therefore, since we have such hope, we act very boldly.* (2 Cor 3:12)

Jesus really threw us a curve when he told us that we are in the world, but not of the world and that the world would hate us as we try to live his way of life. It takes courage and conviction to dare to be different from the world in which we live. On many occasions we will have to "act very boldly."

Some people will consider us foolish for not enjoying life on their level, others will be encouraged by our conviction to follow the Lord. Our courage and daring spring from the gift of hope which the Spirit has implanted in our hearts.

To keep ourselves walking that straight and narrow way, we might often ask ourselves: "What am I doing today that only a Christian would do?"

24 *Our hope for you is firm, for we know that as you share in the sufferings, you also share in the encouragement.* (2 Cor 1:7)

That God is at work in our lives through "thick and thin" is a truth we believe, but of which we need constantly to be reminded. His "TLC" at all times gives us hope and encouragement.

The Holy Spirit, dwelling within us, transforms our faltering steps by raising our hopes and helping us trust the Lord when sufferings come our way. He also assures us that our attitude can effect those around us who need confirmation in their lives.

Holy Spirit, even in reversals when our sense of well-being is jarred, please help us to surmount all difficulties by enkindling our hope and confidence.

25 *It bears all things, believes all things, hopes all things, endures all things.* (1 Cor 13:7)

The Holy Spirit is the source of all love. "The love of God has been poured out into our hearts through the holy Spirit that has been given to us" (Rom 5:5). As one of his many gifts, the Spirit empowers us to "hope all things." With our hope bolstered by love, we will be able to "believe all things and to endure all things."

For the Spirit to empower us, we must be completely receptive to his inspirations and leadings.

Holy Spirit, when our vision is blurred and when we are reluctant to respond to your leadings, stir up your gift of hope within us that we may proceed confidently and joyously through the maze of each day.

26 *Therefore, do not throw away your confidence; it will have great recompense. You need endurance to do the will of God and receive what he has promised.* (Heb 10:35-36)

Pope John Paul II said recently: "If we look only at ourselves, with our limitations and sins, we quickly give way to sadness and discouragement. But if we keep our eyes fixed on the Lord, then our hearts are filled with hope."

When Jesus said: "Without me you can do nothing," he was also saying that with him we can do all things. This truth gives us confidence and trust as we struggle up and down the hills and valleys of life. It gives us hope to pick ourselves up after we have sinned.

Holy Spirit, your inspired word brings hope into every area of our lives. Continue to strengthen our hope, our trust, and our confidence in you.

27 *If there is any encouragement in Christ, any solace in love, any participation in the Spirit, any compassion and mercy, complete my joy by being of the same mind, with the same love, united in heart, thinking one thing.* (Phil 2:1-2)

The outpouring of divine love upon us will free us from many of our shortcomings, mold and transform our thinking, and unite us more closely with one another in mind and heart. Christianity is essentially communitarian and by our "participation in the Spirit," we will be formed into the family of God.

This is the hope and desire of every human heart, since each of us wants to be loved and accepted by others. Our trust in the power of the Holy Spirit working with us will help us strive for this goal.

"Guide me in your truth and teach me, / for you are God my saviour, / and for you I wait all the day" (Ps 25:5).

28 *My eager expectation and hope is that I shall not be put to shame in any way, but that with all boldness, now as always, Christ will be magnified in my body, whether by life or by death.* (Phil 1:20)

Paul's prayer is filled with hope and expectation. Strengthened by the Holy Spirit, he prays that whatever may happen to him will give glory to God and be an example and encouragement to all the followers of the Lord.

Since we are followers of the Lord, many eyes are fixed on us to gauge our reactions to all the vicissitudes of life. Our hope and confidence in the Lord will influence others greatly.

Holy Spirit, enlighten, guide, direct, and strengthen us that "Christ be magnified" in all we do. Then peace and joy will be ours.

29

May the God of hope fill you with all joy and peace in believing, so that you may abound in hope by the power of the holy Spirit.
(Rom 15:13)

Jesus promised us that the Holy Spirit would remain with us always. He also told us that the Spirit would not come empty-handed, but would fill us with all the gifts and graces we need. Our basic need, along with faith and love, is hope. Without hope, we would make little or no effort to live a way of life to which we are called.

As we strive to "abound in hope by the power of the Holy Spirit," we will experience peace and joy—those special fruits of the Spirit. The psalmist gives us some wholesome advice: "Look to him that you may be radiant with joy, / and your faces may not blush with shame" (Ps 34:6).

O Holy Spirit, assist us in keeping our focus always on you, that we may be radiant with joy.

30 *For through the Spirit, by faith, we await the hope of righteousness.* (Gal 5:5)

In his last discourse as Jesus prepared to leave us, he promised to send the Holy Spirit to teach us everything and lead us to all truth. This promise gives us much hope of attaining our eternal destiny.

Aware of our many faults and failings, we recognize how much we need the power of the Holy Spirit if we are to attain righteousness. Our fond hope of being saved is bolstered by the words of St. Paul: "For by grace you have been saved through faith, and this is not from you; it is the gift of God" (Eph 2:8).

Come, Holy Spirit, support our every step with your presence, your power, and your grace.

HOLY TRINITY

31 *He saved us through the bath of rebirth / and renewal by the holy Spirit, / whom he richly poured out on us / through Jesus Christ our savior, / so that we might be justified by his grace / and become heirs in hope of eternal life.*

(Ti 3:5-7)

St. Paul sums up all the reasons for the hope that should dominate our lives. The Father so loved us that he gave us his only

Son to redeem us. By his death and resurrection Jesus completed his role as Redeemer. The Holy Spirit was then "poured out on us" to purify and sanctify us and thus prepare us for the gift of eternal life.

The better we understand the Trinitarian love of the Father, Son, and Holy Spirit for us, the stronger will be our hope of attaining our eternal salvation. The greater our hope, the more pleasing we become to our gracious God.

Joy, Hallmark of a Christian

Come let us sing joyfully to the LORD . . .
(Ps 95:1)

FATHER

1 *I sought the LORD, and he answered me / and delivered me from all my fears. / Look to him that you may be radiant with joy, / and your faces may not blush with shame.* (Ps 34:5-6)

Were we to pause to recall how the providential love of our gracious Father cares for us at every moment of the day, our hearts would overflow with joy and gratitude for all his goodness. He protects us as we maneuver through heavy traffic, as we fly to a distant destination, as we face threatening viruses.

He takes away our fears and worries and fills us with trust and confidence. He guides our way and lightens our step. What joy is ours in knowing that our Father loves us.

Taste and see how good the LORD is;
    happy the man who takes refuge in
    him. (Ps 34:9)

2 *For to whatever man he sees fit he gives
wisdom and knowledge and joy . . .* (Eccl 2:26)

Our Father is such a gentle God. He
knows all our needs, but he does not impose
himself on us. He gives us the wisdom to
recognize our dependence upon him and
the knowledge to use well the gifts he
bestows so generously on us.

As we grow in our appreciation of his
providential care and concern, joy will per-
meate our whole being. It will be a quiet,
interior kind of joy filled with praise and
gratitude.

But the just rejoice and exult before God;
    they are glad and rejoice. (Ps 68:4)

3 *I have trusted in the Eternal God for your
welfare, and joy has come to me from the Holy
One. . . .* (Bar 4:22)

Love always elicits a trust in the person
we love. As our love for our heavenly Father
matures, we will be able to place implicit
confidence in him come what may. This
pleases him very much.

The Lord also assures us: "For I know well

the plans I have in mind for you, . . . plans for your welfare, not for woe'' (Jer 29:11). Our Father responds quickly to our trust and confidence by caring for all our needs. His care and concern fills us with joy.

> Happy he whose help is the God of Jacob,
> whose hope is in the LORD, his God.
> (Ps 146:5)

4 *Then will I go into the altar of God, / the God of my gladness and joy; / Then will I give you thanks upon the harp, / O God, my God!* (Ps 43:4)

From ancient times the altar was always considered the meeting place with God. There people came to celebrate a memorial, to express praise and thanks, to implore aid of the all-good God in all their trials and burdens.

Our altar today is more than a table for worship. The Lord is present Eucharistically to unite himself with us as he gathers our praise and thanks, our sorrow and regret, our petitions and invocations, to present them to the Father in our name. It seems incomprehensible, yet our oblation touches the throne of God. What joy this privilege brings to us.

> I rejoiced because they said to me,
> "We will go up to the house of the LORD."
> (Ps 122:1)

5 *May he grant you joy of heart / and may peace abide among you.* (Sir 50:23)

The dictionary defines joy as the prospect of possessing what we desire. How much greater is Christian joy, since we know that we already possess God's divine life within us and that we have the prospect of receiving a total influx of this life when he brings us to his eternal home.

Christian joy is not merely the absence of sorrow, but an awareness of the presence of the Lord with us. In fact, one of the proofs cited for the existence of God is the joy we find in the thought that God does actually exist.

Lord, grant us the joy of heart that we, as your followers, should reflect in all that we do.

Sing to the LORD a new song
of praise in the assembly of the faithful.
(Ps 149:1)

6 *Those whom the LORD has ransomed will return / and enter Zion singing, / crowned with everlasting joy; / They will meet with joy and gladness, / sorrow and mourning will flee.*
(Is 35:10)

These prophetic words are being fulfilled in our times. Jesus came "to give his life as a ransom for many" (Mt 20:28). We are destined to enter into the heavenly Zion, where we will be crowned with everlasting joy.

St. John affirms this prophecy as he records his own vision: "He will wipe every tear from their eyes, and there shall be no more death or mourning, wailing or pain, [for] the old order has passed away" (Rv 21:4). This hope and promise fills us with a joy no one can take from us.

> Happy are they who observe what is right,
> who do always what is just. (Ps 106:3)

7 *Give me back the joy of your salvation, and a willing spirit sustain in me.* (Ps 51:14)

We are all sinners in the sight of God. St. Paul expresses our own lament when he says: "For I do not do the good I want, but I do the evil I do not want" (Rom 7:19). The awareness of our sins can become a heavy burden for us. A sense of shame and guilt can rob us of the joy which we all desire.

However, the knowledge that our Father is a God of mercy and compassion, eager and anxious to wipe out our offenses, is the source of incomparable joy. This awareness gives us back the joy of our salvation.

> Happy are you who fear the LORD,
> who walk in his ways! (Ps 128:1)

8 *The lowly will ever find joy in the LORD, and the poor rejoice in the Holy One of Israel.*

(Is 29:19)

Among some of the ancient Hebrews, poverty and illness were considered an indication of God's displeasure with a person. That person was often considered to be a grave sinner. Even today many think of illness or misfortune as a direct punishment from God. Although at times God may capitalize on some problem area in our life to remind us that he must be the prime focus in our life, this is hardly meant as a direct punishment.

Jesus changed such thinking when he reached out in loving concern to the sick and suffering, the poor and downtrodden. The lowly and the poor are very precious to the Lord. In turn, they find great joy and rejoicing in his loving concern.

At your name they rejoice all the day,
and through your justice they are
exalted. (Ps 89:17)

9 *I rejoice heartily in the LORD, / in my God is the joy of my soul; / For he has clothed me with the robe of salvation, / and wrapped me in the mantle of justice, . . .* (Is 61:10)

Every human being is endowed by God with a desire to be accepted and loved. Within the heart of every person there is a longing for genuine happiness. Experience teaches us that only partial, and sometimes short-lived, happiness can be attained in this life.

Our faith holds out great promise for us. We believe that our loving Father wants to clothe us with the "robe of salvation," which is perfect happiness with him in our eternal home. This conviction makes us rejoice heartily knowing that the Lord is faithful to his promises. This is genuine joy.

> Happy the man who fears the LORD,
>   who greatly delights in his commands.
> (Ps 112:1)

10 *"With joy you will draw water / at the fountain of salvation, / and say on that day: / Give thanks to the LORD, acclaim his name. . . ."* (Is 12:3-4)

This comforting prophecy assured the people down through the ages that eternal happiness awaited them. These prophetic words have been fulfilled in these Christian times. Jesus is the source of salvation. He is the inexhaustible fountain from which the living water of his divine life flows into our hearts.

Even if we have the misfortune of turning away from him at times, we can always return to find him more than anxious to receive us if we are humbly disposed. This realization fills our heart with thanks and joy.

> Sing to the LORD with thanksgiving;
> sing praise with the harp to our God.
>
> (Ps 147:7)

SON

11 ... "My soul proclaims the greatness of the Lord; / /my spirit rejoices in God my savior." (Lk 1:46-47)

The angel's announcement to Mary must have confused and bewildered her. Only after her faith was confirmed by Elizabeth was she able to rejoice and glorify God.

In her profound humanity, Mary ascribed to God all that was happening. She rejoiced also that the world was not to be redeemed after these ages of waiting. Her heart thrilled at the goodness of the Lord, and her heart sang out his praise in her joyful hymn, the Magnificat.

As we rejoice with Mary, may our hearts thank God for the gift of his Son and also thank Mary for saying yes to our salvation.

"Praise the LORD, O my soul" (Ps 146:1).

12 *The angel said to them, "Do not be afraid; for behold, I proclaim to you good news of great joy that will be for all the people. For today in the city of David a savior has been born for you who is Messiah and Lord."* (Lk 2:10-11)

The angel's announcement to the shepherds of the birth of Jesus was the fulfillment of a promise and prophecy made down through the centuries. It was the long-awaited answer to myriad prayers from countless hearts. Little wonder that it brought much joy to a waiting world.

Each year our hearts are joyous and light as we celebrate Christmas because we realize that "God so loved the world that he gave his only Son . . ." (Jn 3:16).

My lips shall shout for joy
    as I sing your praises;
My soul also, which you have redeemed.
                                (Ps 71:23)

13 *". . . I tell you, there will be rejoicing among the angels of God over one sinner who repents."* (Lk 15:10)

When a certain part of our human body is in pain, the whole body suffers. This is also true of the body of Christ. We are the body of Christ along with all the saints, and all our brothers and sisters throughout the world.

We are all affected when a brother or sister goes astray.

The Lord is greatly pleased when a wayward son or daughter returns to him. He asks: "Do I not rather rejoice when he turns from his evil way that he may live?" (Ez 18:23). Even the angels of God rejoice "over one sinner who repents."

> But I will rejoice in the LORD,
>   I will be joyful because of his salvation.
>   (Ps 35:9)

14 *"So you also are now in anguish. But I will see you again, and your hearts will rejoice, and no one will take your joy away from you."*
                                              (Jn 16:22)

Jesus assures us that our anguish or suffering would eventually be turned into great joy, since he is dwelling with us and within us. He promised: "I will not leave you orphans, I will come to you" (Jn 14:18). He came to make his permanent abode with us at the moment of our baptism.

His indwelling with the outpouring of his love upon us is the cause of genuine joy for us.

> For you made him a blessing forever;
>   you gladdened him with the joy of your
>   presence. (Ps 21:7)

15 *"I have told you this so that my joy might be in you and your joy might be complete."*
(Jn 15:11)

The central theme in the Gospel which Jesus revealed to us is the truth that the Father loves us with an infinite love. Jesus' own love for us is equally great. Knowing such an overwhelming love will motivate us to respond with greater love and generosity to the will of the Lord in our lives.

The awareness of God's love and our attempt to respond in love will be the source of great joy for us. Thank you, Lord, for making our joy so complete with this reassuring teaching,

> Happy the nation whose God is the LORD, the people he has chosen for his own inheritance. (Ps 33:12)

16 *". . . There will be more joy in heaven over one sinner who repents than over ninety-nine righteous people who have no need of repentance."* (Lk 15:7)

Jesus is in his glory, but what is his glory? The glory of Jesus is the continuing of his redemptive work on earth. When we come to him with our sinfulness, it makes him happy because we are recognizing him for what he wants to be most—our Savior and

Redeemer. He is delighted to welcome sinners on their return and touch them with his forgiving, healing love.

The psalmist reminds us that the Lord's forgiveness brings peace and joy to a contrite heart.

> Happy is he whose fault is taken away,
>   whose sin is covered.
> Happy the man to whom the LORD
>   imputes not guilt,
>   in whose spirit there is no guile.
>
> (Ps 32:1, 2)

17 *"But now I am coming to you. I speak this in the world so that they may share my joy completely."* (Jn 17:13)

In his prayer at the Last Supper, Jesus prayed that we would always be closely united with him. With eyes raised heavenward, he asked the Father: "that they may all be one, as you, Father, are in me and I in you, that they also may be in us" (Jn 17:21).

We become one with Jesus when he shares his divine life with us, and the Father adopts us as his children. This unique and intimate union with the Godhead is the source of great joy for us.

> Happy they who dwell in your house!
>   continually they praise you. (Ps 84:5)

18 *While they were still incredulous for joy and were amazed, he asked them, "Have you anything here to eat?"* (Lk 24:41)

Luke's Gospel abounds with messianic joy. This appearance of Jesus to the apostles on the very day of the resurrection was no exception. The apostles could not grasp what they saw with their eyes, but they were thrilled that he was alive.

They were also filled with joy because his coming to them was a healing presence. Just a few days earlier they deserted him in "his hour." They must have experienced a sense of guilt. His appearance to them with loving concern was a way of telling them that all was forgiven. His forgiving presence with us is always accompanied with much peace and joy.

This is the day the LORD has made;
let us be glad and rejoice in it. (Ps 118:24)

19 *They did him homage and then returned to Jerusalem with great joy.* (Lk 24:52)

Jesus had just left his apostles and ascended into heaven. They would never see him again in bodily form. Yet they returned to the Upper Room filled with joy. They witnessed his divinity and began to realize, with the enlightenment of the Holy Spirit, that he was "indescribably more present in his divinity than in his humanity'' (St. Leo the Great).

When we understand that Jesus is more present to us in his divinity than he could ever be if he were only bodily present among us, our joy, like that of the disciples, will know no bounds. We are a privileged people.

> How lovely is your dwelling place,
> O LORD of hosts! (Ps 84:2)

20 *Although you have not seen him you love him; even though you do not see him now yet believe in him, you rejoice with an indescribable and glorious joy, as you attain the goal of [your] faith, the salvation of your souls.* (1 Pt 1:8-9)

Faith is knowing with our hearts what our minds cannot quite comprehend. This kind of faith is closely related to and dependent upon love. Faith enables us to place our trust and confidence in the person we love. Jesus always pleaded for faith in himself.

The "goal of our faith" is the happiness of heaven. Jesus asks for our faith and trust in him and his promise of salvation. Such a faith is pleasing to the Lord and it fills us with "an indescribable and glorious joy."

> O LORD of hosts,
> happy the men who trust in you!
> (Ps 84:13)

HOLY SPIRIT

21 *"You have made known to me the paths of life; you will fill me with joy in your presence."* (Acts 2:28)

Jesus came to reveal to us the path of life he wants us to follow. He also knew that without divine help we can easily stray. For this reason he sent the Holy Spirit to enlighten and guide us along this path of life. He assured us that the Holy Spirit would always remain with us and within us (cf Jn 14:17).

Pausing to remember that the Holy Spirit is abiding with us brings great joy to our hearts. We not only have the assurance that we are on the right path, but his loving presence sustains us as we journey.

Let them make thank offerings
and declare his works with shouts of
joy. (Ps 107:22)

22 *. . . They were all filled with the holy Spirit and began to speak in different tongues, as the Spirit enabled them to proclaim.* (Acts 2:4)

The disciples were ecstatic with joy when they were filled with the Holy Spirit on Pentecost. Since they were eager to share the joy of redemption, the Holy Spirit miraculously endowed them with languages which they had not learned, but which foreigners understood.

As we permit the Holy Spirit to fill us with his love, peace, and joy, we too will feel compelled to share the good news. Nor need we be concerned what to say and do, for the Spirit will guide us to evangelize if we are open to his divine influence.

Come, let us sing joyfully to the LORD;
  let us acclaim the Rock of our salvation.
(Ps 95:1)

23 *In contrast, the fruit of the Spirit is love, joy, peace, patience, kindness, generosity, faithfulness.* (Gal 5:22)

Joy is that fruit of the Holy Spirit which helps us to serve God cheerfully. As we strive to look beyond ourselves and our personal desires, we can more easily recognize God's plan for us. Our yes becomes easier, and we will find joy in this frame of mind.

We have all had an experience of enduring a seemingly tragic reversal in our life, only to discover some time later that it was a blessing. The Holy Spirit creates a feeling of satisfaction and fulfillment within us which is the cause of much joy.

Give me back the joy of your salvation,
  and a willing spirit sustain in me.
(Ps 51:14)

24 *With all prayer and supplication, pray at every opportunity in the Spirit. . . .*

(Eph 6:18)

Prayer has a unique power and importance. It is a source of much joy. The joy experienced in prayer is not necessarily an ecstatic kind of joy, but essentially a spiritual joy. Even though we may be suffering serious affliction, we can still experience joy.

Just as we can be at peace even though we are in pain, so we can also have quiet, supernatural joy even though we are assailed by many problems. The Holy Spirit's gift of joy is one of the many fruits of fervent prayer.

Praise the LORD, all you nations;
    glorify him, all you peoples! (Ps 117:1)

25 *And you became imitators of us and of the Lord, receiving the word in great affliction, with joy from the holy Spirit.* (1 Thes 1:6)

Living the Word of God requires some self-denial and dedication. Jesus asks us to take up our cross daily and follow in his footsteps. To some, this way of life might seem too restrictive, and they hesitate or even refuse to accept the invitation of the Lord. Paradoxically, the more we give, the greater our joy becomes.

The Holy Spirit encourages us to look beyond our selfish concerns to discover that it is more blessed to give than to receive.

This giving is always accompanied with great peace and joy.

> Let the heavens be glad and the earth rejoice; . . .
> > let the plains be joyful and all that is in them! (Ps 96:11-12)

26 *It (love) does not rejoice over wrongdoing but rejoices with the truth.* (1 Cor 13:6)

The Holy Spirit is the very essence and source of divine love which he shares with us. "The love of God has been poured out into our hearts through the holy Spirit that has been given to us" (Rom 5:5). Love wants to do everything which will please and avoid anything which will displease the person loved.

Love creates within us a desire for the good, the holy, and the innocent and does not rejoice in wrongdoing. An important component of love is that joy which only the Holy Spirit can give.

> Fill us at daybreak with your kindness,
> > that we may shout for joy and gladness all our days. (Ps 90:14)

27 *If [one] part suffers, all the parts suffer with it; if one part is honored, all the parts share its joy.* (1 Cor 12:26)

When we suffer from a severe headache, our whole body feels miserable. The same is true of our spiritual body, which is the family of God. The Holy Spirit builds Christian community with love as its binding force. This realization should create a spirit of compassion within us for all our brothers and sisters who may be suffering.

Likewise, we should be filled with great joy when some member of our spiritual family is honored. Love leaves no room for envy, jealousy, or disappointment, only for joy and rejoicing. Elizabeth rejoiced at Mary's good fortune. To the consternation of his disciples, John the Baptist also rejoiced when Jesus attracted followers.

Happy the people who know the joyful shout;
in the light of your countenance, O LORD, they walk. (Ps 89:16)

28 *The disciples were filled with joy and the holy Spirit.* (Acts 13:52)

When the angel announced the birth of Jesus to the shepherds, he emphasized joy: "Behold, I proclaim to you good news of great joy that will be for all the people" (Lk

2:10). As Jesus' teaching ministry was drawing to a close, he exclaimed: "I have told you this so that my joy might be in you and your joy might be complete" (Jn 15:11).

When Paul and Barnabas proclaimed the good news, the Spirit filled the disciples with joy. As the Word of God finds a home in our hearts, we too, will experience the genuine joy of the Holy Spirit.

> Sing joyfully to the LORD, all you lands;
> break into song; sing praise. (Ps 98:4)

29 *Rejoice in the Lord always. I shall say it again: rejoice!* (Phil 4:4)

The Holy Spirit shares his gift of joy with us and urges us to manifest this joy in all of our daily living. We are all striving for holiness and we need to recall that there has never been a sad saint. In fact, the process for canonization states that a candidate "should have displayed an expansive joy in his/her life and influence, however melancholy his/her natural temperament may have been."

St. Paul urges us to rejoice in the Lord always, regardless of what predicament we may seem to be in. Throughout the psalms we also find admonitions to be joyous.

> Sing joyfully to the LORD, all you lands;
> serve the LORD with gladness;
> come before him with joyful song.
> (Ps 100:1-2)

30 *... "Alleluia! / The Lord has established his reign, / [our] God the almighty. / Let us rejoice and be glad / and give him glory. ..."*
(Rv 19:6-7)

Repeatedly Pope Paul VI reminded us that we Christians have a special mission of reflecting the joy of the Holy Spirit in our lives. He wrote an apostolic exhortation which pointed out the need for joy in the hearts of all persons and for the special joy which every Christian should radiate.

We can become crucifixion Christians instead of resurrection Christians. Sometimes we are so busy backing away from hell that we miss the joy of going to heaven. Our joy is founded on the fact that the Holy Spirit has established his reign in our hearts and we are destined, with his help, to reach the perfect joy of heaven.

The LORD is king; let the earth rejoice;
    let the many isles be glad. (Ps 97:1)

HOLY TRINITY

31 *Rejoice always. Pray without ceasing. In all circumstances give thanks, for this is the will of God for you in Christ Jesus. Do not quench the Spirit.* (1 Thes 5:16-19)

Prayer is our privileged communication with the Father, Son, and Holy Spirit, which deepens our relationship with all three Divine Persons. The more prayerful we become, the more grateful we will be for all the Lord's blessings. This is the Father's will for us.

We cannot thank the Lord as we ought; hence we call on Jesus to join us in thanking the Father. The Spirit, too, sustains and deepens our relationship if we do not quench his working within us.

> Trust in him at all times, O my people!
>   Pour out your hearts before him;
>   God is our refuge! (Ps 62:9)

Peace, a Divine Gift

. . . May grace and peace be yours in abundance. (1 Pt 1:2)

FATHER

1 *So Gideon built there an altar to the LORD and called it Yahweh-shalom. . . ." [God is peace]* (Jgs 6:24)

John tried to describe God's infinite perfection by saying "God is love," while Gideon uses the title "God is peace."

"God is love" and "God is peace." We are created in the image and likeness of God and share in his divine nature. We, too, long for love and peace.

We will enjoy great peace when we have an intimate, personal relationship with God our loving Father. We build this relationship when we respond to his love by striving to fulfill his will at all times in our lives.

2 *I will make with them a covenant of peace; it shall be an everlasting covenant with them, and I will multiply them, and put my sanctuary among them forever.* (Ez 37:26)

A covenant is a solemn, binding agreement made between two parties. The Lord used the word covenant to underline his fidelity to his promise and to encourage us to fulfill our part of the covenant agreement.

Since God is peace itself, his very presence within us is a sanctuary, an inexhaustible source of peace, if we are receptive to his gift of peace.

Thank you, Father, for your abiding peace within me.

3 *Those who love your law have great peace, and for them there is no stumbling block.*
(Ps 119:165)

Peace is the fruit of an intimate, personal, loving relationship with God our Father. We must be convinced in our very bones that God means it when he says he loves us, that we are the apple of his eye.

We enjoy great peace when we keep his law. This is the ideal way for us to express our love for him; it will also lead us to the eternal peace of heaven.

4 *May he grant you joy of heart / and may peace abide among you; / May his goodness toward us endure in Israel / as long as the heavens are above.* (Sir 50:23-24)

Peace is a God-given gift which brings us many blessings abounding from the goodness of the Lord. His peace will:

—free us from worry and anxiety
—strengthen our faith and trust in the Lord
—bring joy, sunshine, smiles, and laughter
—eliminate discouragement and frustration
—help us see the good in others
—lighten our burdens
—highlight the beauty of the world around us
—encourage us to praise and thank our wonderful God and Father.

5 *Better a dry crust with peace / than a house full of feasting with strife.* (Prv 17:1)

With materialism rampant in our times, we are prone to regard worldly possessions as the source of peace and contentment. Sad to say, many people who have spent long, hard years striving to accumulate material comforts and conveniences, have only been disillusioned in their pursuit of happiness.

Our personal relationship with the Lord is

the only source of genuine peace. Whether we are blessed with worldly goods or not, the spirit of detachment is the only source of real peace.

With peace in our hearts, even a crust of bread tastes good.

6 *But the meek shall possess the land, / they shall delight in abounding peace.* (Ps 37:11)

A meek person has a mild temperament and is not apt to take offense or be hurt by some unimportant casual remark. Meekness is closely allied with humility, poverty, and lowliness. Meekness is one of the fruits of the Holy Spirit.

A meek person is sometimes erroneously considered a weak, spiritless, passive kind of person. Quite the contrary is true.

In the Beatitudes, Jesus assures us that a meek person will enter heaven to enjoy eternal peace.

7 *"A nation of firm purpose you keep in peace; / in peace, for its trust in you." / Trust in the LORD forever! / For the LORD is an eternal Rock.* (Is 26:3-4)

We are filled with peace when we place all our confidence and trust in God. In turn, confidence and trust in God is the fruit of knowing God with our heart as a kind, gracious, loving God who cares for us at every moment of the day; a merciful Father who is eager and anxious to forgive all our sinfulness; a powerful healer who remedies all our sorrows, pains, and wounds.

This awareness gives us a "firm purpose" in life and brings genuine peace.

8 *. . . My love shall never leave you / nor my covenant of peace be shaken, / says the LORD, who has mercy on you.* (Is 54:10)

Our gracious Father made a solemn promise that his covenant of peace would never be shaken. Sin alone can destroy or prevent our hearts from enjoying his peace. He restores to us this peace by forgiving and healing us of any sinfulness when we come to him with a contrite heart and a humble spirit.

Contemplating his mercy and compassion will fill us with the peace which his presence brings us.

9 *But the souls of the just are in the hand of God, / and no torment shall touch them. / They seemed, in the view of the foolish, to be dead; / and their passing away was thought an affliction / and their going forth from us, utter destruction. / But they are in peace.* (Wis 3:1-3)

Death is the doorway through which we must pass to enter into the eternal peace of heaven. The fear of the unknown may cause us some anxiety, but the love of the Lord bids us to trust him.

We can well imagine how eagerly Mary, our mother, longed to be reunited with her Son in heaven. Let us ask her to obtain that same grace for us.

10 *"The LORD bless you and keep you! / The LORD let his face shine upon you, / and be gracious to you! / The LORD look upon you kindly and give you peace!"* (Nm 6:24-26)

In this composite of blessings, peace is rightly listed last because it represents the culmination of all other blessings: our eternal salvation in which we will enjoy perfect peace forever.

This special blessing, inspired by the Holy Spirit, serves as a perfect parting greeting to family and friends. It would be an ideal custom to adopt.

The peace of the Lord be with you.

SON

11 *He shall stand firm and shepherd his flock / by the strength of the LORD / in the majestic name of the LORD, his God; / And they shall remain, for now his greatness / shall reach to the ends of the earth; / he shall be peace. . . .* (Mi 5:3-4)

Every minute detail of the redemptive mission of Jesus has been foretold which proves the Father's caring love for us. He meticulously planned every phase of our redemption to convince us of his boundless forgiving, healing love.

Lord, may we praise and glorify your "majestic name" every day of our lives. May the ceaseless praise of the heavenly hosts ring in our hearts always.

12 *"... The daybreak [Messiah] from on high will visit us ... to guide our feet into the path of peace."* (Lk 1:78-79)

Jesus guides our feet into the path of peace by outlining the way of life we are to live. It is summed up in two laws: love God first and foremost, and love your neighbor as yourself.

Striving to love in this way will build good personal relationships, from which love will flow as from an inexhaustible fountain.

Lord, teach us how to love, and guide our feet along the path to genuine peace.

13 *... "Daughter, your faith has saved you. Go in peace and be cured of your affliction."* (Mk 5:34)

This woman, with a long-standing illness, had great faith in Jesus. She believed that a simple touch of his garment would heal her. Her faith was fully rewarded as Jesus healed her and brought her great peace. She felt that Jesus cared enough about her to relieve her suffering. Jesus responded to her great faith.

Lord Jesus, grant us the grace to grow in faith and trust in you that we, too, may enjoy that peace which only you can give.

14 *"Blessed are the peacemakers, / for they will be called children of God."* (Mt 5:9)

We become peacemakers by manifesting our loving concern for others. We do so more by what we are than by what we do and say. If our confidence and trust in the Lord are reflected in our attitudes and actions, and if our lives radiate the peace and joy of the Lord, we will be effective peacemakers.

Lord Jesus, fill us with that peace which the world cannot give, so that we may strive to bring your peace to others, and on the day you call us to yourself, may go forward joyfully to meet you, the Prince of Peace.

15 . . .*"Your faith has saved you; go in peace."* (Lk 7:50)

The sinful woman was a miserable, unhappy person. In utter desperation she placed her hope in Jesus, seeking some sort of relief and comfort. Recognizing her plight, Jesus responded to her innermost need by forgiving her completely.

Sin fragments and destroys the peace the Lord wants us to enjoy. If we have failed him, we have only to remember how eager Jesus is to forgive and heal us, when we acknowledge our waywardness and seek his mercy and compassion. Then we, too, will hear those comforting words:

"Your sins are forgiven; go in peace."

16 *"Jerusalem, Jerusalem, you who kill the prophets and stone those sent to you, how many times I yearned to gather your children together as a hen gathers her brood under her wings, but you were unwilling!"* (Lk 13:34)

Jesus came as the Redeemer to offer eternal peace and salvation to everyone, but many of his own people refused to believe in him. With great sorrow Jesus lamented their reaction, not simply because they rejected him, but also because they refused to accept the eternal salvation he was offering them.

Today we, too, have freedom to refuse many of the Lord's gifts. He offers them, but he does not compel us to accept them, nor does he force us to use his gifts to attain great peace.

Jesus, have we caused you to lament over our indifference or even rejection?

17 *"Peace I leave with you; my peace I give to you. Not as the world gives do I give it to you. . . ."* (Jn 14:27)

On the eve of his sacrificial death, Jesus promised that the all-important fruit of his redeeming love would be Shalom, the gift of salvation.

"Salvation itself is nothing else but peace—*shalom*, the high point of all messianic promises and of the whole work of Christ." (Rene Laurentin, *Is the Virgin Appearing at Medjugorje?*, [Gaithersburg, MD, The Word Among Us Press, 1984] p. 62)

Lord, grant us that peace in this life which will lead us to eternal peace.

18 *For in him all the fullness was pleased to dwell, and through him to reconcile all things for him, making peace by the blood of his cross. . . .* (Col 1:19-20)

By pouring out his blood on the cross and rising triumphantly from the tomb, Jesus was able to share his divine life and love with us. This is the peace he promised. It is the peace which culminates in eternal salvation. This is the peace we pray for at Mass:

"Lord Jesus Christ, you said to your apostles, I leave you peace, my peace I give you. Look not on our sins, but on the faith of your church and grant us the peace and unity of your kingdom where you live forever and ever. Amen."

19 ... *"Peace be with you."* (Jn 20:19)

When Jesus appeared to the apostles in the Upper Room on the day of the resurrection, his very presence brought them much comfort in the midst of the pain they were experiencing because they thought they had lost him forever. His loving concern and his prayerful greeting: "Peace be with you," removed the feelings of guilt they were suffering for deserting him in his hour of need.

Jesus is dwelling with us and within us, assuring us of the same forgiving, healing love when we disappoint him. Listen as he says: "I forgive you. Peace be with you."

20 ... *"Peace be with you. . . ."* (Jn 20:21)

By his death and resurrection Jesus redeemed the whole human race—every person who ever lived, who is living now, and who ever will live. Jesus loves each one of us personally and individually and wants to assure us of his pardon and peace. To this end he instituted the Sacrament of Reconciliation in which we could encounter him personally to receive his forgiveness and healing, his pardon and peace.

Lord, may we rejoice in your peace forever.

HOLY SPIRIT

21 *He came and preached peace to you who were far off and peace to those who were near, for through him we both have access in one Spirit to the Father.* (Eph 2:17-18)

Jesus came into the world to proclaim the good news of God's love for us which will lead us to Shalom—salvation. After gaining that peace for us by his redemptive death and resurrection, Jesus handed over the work of sanctification to the Holy Spirit.

Jesus promised that he would not leave us orphans but that he would send the Holy Spirit who "will teach you everything and remind you of all that [I] told you" (Jn 14:26). This truth is the source of peace in this life and a guarantee of that peace, which has no end or limit.

22 *... The fruit of the Spirit is love, joy, peace, patience, kindness, generosity, faithfulness, gentleness, self-control. ...* (Gal 5:22-23)

Peace is a precious gift of the Holy Spirit. It is a comprehensive gift since it includes all the other blessings of the Lord. Peace is the crowning blessing of Jesus' redemptive work.

When we strive, aided by the sanctifying presence of the Holy Spirit to avoid sin in our lives, to endeavor to follow the will of the Lord and to reach out in loving concern to others, we will enjoy God's gift of peace.

Holy Spirit, grant us your gift of peace.

23 *And the fruit of righteousness is sown in peace for those who cultivate peace.*

(Jas 3:18)

The work of sanctification is ascribed in a special way to the Holy Spirit. He leads us to holiness by enkindling within us a desire to love God and be loved by him. He enlightens us with the gift of discernment, enabling us to recognize the will of God in our lives. He draws us into prayer since "we do not know how to pray as we ought."

In our quiet prayer time these inspirations and motivations from the Holy Spirit will become more evident. Then we will know genuine peace and be assured of that perfect peace which is eternal.

24 *May mercy, peace, and love be yours in abundance.* (Jude 1:2)

This prayerful greeting fills our hearts with a joy beyond description. The Holy Spirit constantly reminds us that his love is infinite and unconditional, and that he wants to forgive us more than we could even want forgiveness. His boundless love is the source of his mercy.

He reminds us that "The love of God has been poured out into our heart, through the holy Spirit that has been given to us" (Rom 5:5).

Divine love awaits our loving response so that we may enjoy peace and love in abundance.

25 *This is how you can know the Spirit of God: every spirit that acknowledges Jesus Christ come in the flesh belongs to God.* (1 Jn 4:2)

Through the presence and power of the Holy Spirit dwelling within us we will come to know God as our loving, gracious Father. Only in knowing him can we come to love him above all things. When we love God we will be able to love ourselves as we are and accept our neighbor as he or she is.

In striving to establish this threefold relationship we will experience genuine peace. The Holy Spirit, dwelling within us, is the very source of love, peace, and joy. He will empower all our striving.

Come, Holy Spirit, help us to be unselfishly concerned about others and keep our eyes only on the good in them.

26 *... Rejoice. Mend your ways, encourage one another, agree with one another, live in peace, and the God of love and peace will be with you.* (2 Cor 13:11)

Many of our ways and endeavors are self-centered. We mend our ways by striving to forget ourselves, and to take an interest in other people and their concerns. Every person, including ourselves, wants to be appreciated.

Be assured that the God of love and peace will fill us with his joy.

27 *So turn from youthful desires and pursue righteousness, faith, love, and peace, along with those who call on the Lord with purity of heart.* (2 Tm 2:22)

When St. Paul advises us, as he did Timothy, to "pursue righteousness, faith, love, and peace," he is encouraging us to pray for and also to exercise these gifts of the Holy Spirit.

As our love for the Lord grows and matures, our faith likewise will become more vibrant and operative. In turn, we will grow in holiness and know a peace which will be a prelude to the eternal peace which the Lord wishes us to enjoy.

Holy Spirit, give us that grace and enlightenment to continue to "pursue."

28 *May the Lord of peace himself give you peace at all times and in every way. The Lord be with all of you.* (2 Thes 3:16)

The Holy Spirit is "the Lord of peace," as he is also the God of love. By his indwelling in us as his special temple, he becomes the source of all our peace.

Keeping ourselves aware of his abiding presence will bring us "peace at all times and in every way."

When we greet one another in Paul's words: "The Lord be with all of you," we are prayerfully extending all the blessings of the Lord, including peace, to one another.

29 *Strive for peace with everyone, and for that holiness without which no one will see the Lord.* (Heb 12:14)

The desire for holiness within the hearts of every one of us is itself a gift from the Holy Spirit. He also helps us to attain genuine peace as a fruit of a good relationship with God, with ourselves, and with our neighbor. This very striving for peace will bring us that holiness which will insure our being with God for all eternity.

Holy Spirit of God, help us to walk in your grace and peace always.

30 *"But you will receive power when the holy Spirit comes upon you, and you will be my witnesses in Jerusalem, throughout Judea and Samaria, and to the ends of the earth."* (Acts 1:8)

Our own peace, like love, is increased and enriched the more we share it with others. Like the apostles we receive power from the Holy Spirit to be witnesses of the Lord's love, peace, and joy to our own family, our community, and far beyond.

O Holy Spirit, keep us on the straight and narrow path, watching over us and guiding us to celestial peace—*shalom.*

HOLY TRINITY

31 *In the foreknowledge of God the Father, through sanctification by the Spirit, for obedience and sprinkling with the blood of Jesus Christ: may grace and peace be yours in abundance.*
(1 Pt 1:2)

Grace and peace are divine gifts showered upon us by the Holy Trinity—Father, Son, and Holy Spirit—as the fruit of our redemption and as preparation for the eternal peace awaiting us in heaven.

We are privileged to join all the angels and saints in heaven in praising, glorifying, and thanking God our Father, Jesus our Savior, and the Holy Spirit our Sanctifier, for the divine gift of peace.

Powerful
Trinitarian Prayer

. . . *"I have eagerly desired to eat this Passover with you. . . ."* (Lk 22:15)

HOLY TRINITY

1 *The grace of the Lord Jesus Christ and the love of God and the fellowship of the holy Spirit be with all of you.* (2 Cor 13:13)

These words of Scripture are used by the celebrant to greet and welcome all who have come to offer the Eucharist. The Mass is the most powerful prayer and the most sublime act of worship we can offer to God. In the Eucharistic celebration, we offer praise, honor, glory, and thanks to all three persons of the Blessed Trinity.

We thank our providing Father for the gift of our natural life as well as the divine life he shares with us by accepting us as members of his family.

245

We thank and praise Jesus as we re-present his redemptive act in which he redeemed our fallen human nature and showed us the way to eternal peace.

We worship the Holy Spirit for abiding within us to purify and sanctify us as we journey onward toward our eternal home-land. The Mass is a Trinitarian prayer in which we worship all three Divine Persons in one God.

Glory be to the Father, and to the Son, and to the Holy Spirit. Amen.

FATHER

2 ... *"Father, I have sinned against heaven and against you; I no longer deserve to be called your son."* (Lk 15:21)

When we approach our heavenly Father, like the prodigal son, we are dismayed by our human faults and failures. As we begin to celebrate the Eucharist with Jesus, our high priest, we are reminded that we have failed the Lord at times by our self-cen-teredness, our lack of generous response to his grace, and in various other ways.

In the Penitential Rite we pause to ask the

Father's forgiveness, so that our gift of self might be more pleasing to him. Our gracious Father cannot turn a deaf ear to our sincere, contrite plea: "Lord, have mercy; Christ, have mercy; Lord, have mercy," followed by the celebrant's fervent prayer for us and for himself:

> May almighty God have mercy on us, forgive our sins, and bring us to everlasting life.

3 *"Glory to God in the highest and on earth peace to those on whom his favor rests."*
(Lk 2:14)

While the entire Mass gives glory and praise to God, we pause to verbalize our praise that it may become a deeper conviction within us. We bring our hymn of praise in the words which the multitude of heavenly hosts sang in announcing the birth of Jesus to the shepherds.

Praise is a high form of prayer and is very pleasing to God. When we praise God, we raise our minds and hearts above ourselves and all our own personal needs to focus on the infinite goodness of our loving Father.

May our hearts often sing: "Glory to God in the highest."

4   *Faith is the realization of what is hoped for and evidence of things not seen.* (Heb 11:1)

After the homily on Sundays and solemnities we make a profession of faith, together with all the worshipers. This is not just a formal recital of all the doctrines we accept and believe in, but instead a prayerful commitment not only to believe what was revealed, but to promise to live according to these truths.

The Lord calls us to a life of faith in him and all that he has revealed. We know how pleased God was with the faith of Abraham and all the other giants of faith in the Old Testament (cf Heb 11). The Gospel relates how much Jesus was pleased when he discovered in his hearers faith in himself and his teachings. His disappointment at a lack of faith was equally evident. The Holy Spirit also calls us to a life of faith and offers faith as one of his special gifts.

May our faith become stronger, more dynamic, and vibrant with each Mass we offer.

5   *That with one accord you may with one voice glorify the God and Father of our Lord Jesus Christ.* (Rom 15:6)

We are one family—God's family. We are a community, all members of the body of Christ. At Mass we praise and glorify our

Father. When we assemble with our brothers and sisters, our praise swells into a mighty crescendo.

When we begin the Preface of the Mass, we are reminded of our duty to thank the Lord for all his benefits. We pause after the Liturgy of the Word to begin the Eucharistic Prayer with these words:

> Father, all powerful and ever-living God, we do well always and everywhere to give you thanks through our Lord Jesus Christ.

We realize that our own gratitude is grossly inadequate. For this reason, we present it to Jesus, who in turn unites it with his own prayer of thanksgiving. This makes the Mass such a powerful prayer.

6 *"He that offers praise as a sacrifice glorifies me; and to him that goes the right way I will show the salvation of God."* (Ps 50:23)

In Eucharistic Prayer I we have an ideal way of offering our praise to the Lord and to fulfill his desire to receive the praise, honor, and glory which we owe to him. We begin the Eucharistic Prayer by announcing our intention to offer our homage to our caring, concerned Father. We know only too well that we cannot praise him adequately our-

250 / *Know Me*

selves; hence we offer our praise and thanks through Jesus our high priest.

God does not need our thanks and praise, but we need to express our duty to honor him. Throughout the liturgy of the Mass we often repeat our praise and thanksgiving.

We come to you Father; with praise and thanksgiving through Jesus Christ your Son. Through him we ask you to accept and bless these gifts we offer in sacrifice.''

(EP I)

7 ... *"Our Father in heaven, / hallowed be your name, / your kingdom come, / your will be done, / on earth as in heaven."* (Mt 6:9-10)

When we pray the Lord's Prayer at Mass, it becomes a more powerful prayer since Jesus is praying with us. We ask the Father to give us the grace to hallow his name and his person. We pray that his kingdom may reign in our hearts and the hearts of all people.

We also ask that we may be able to do his will as perfectly as Jesus did. Jesus fulfilled the Father's will exactly, since love does everything to please the person loved. As we pray we can ask for the grace to manifest our love by obeying his will as it is obeyed in heaven.

Slowly and reflectively let us pray: "Our Father, who art in heaven . . .''

8 *"Give us each day our daily bread."* (Lk 11:3)

When we speak of bread in scriptural language, it means all our needs. Our provident Father wants to give us all we need.

At Mass, in union with the whole assembled community, we ask him to continue his beneficence upon us and the world as we pray: "Give us each day our daily bread."

Jesus told us that the Father knows all our needs and is eager to supply them, but that he waits for us to ask him. In presenting our petitions we acknowledge our own poverty and our dependence upon him. As we verbalize our requests, it purifies our desires lest we become too self-centered.

May our gratefulness increase with each passing day.

9 *But God, who is rich in mercy, because of the great love he had for us, even when we were dead in our transgressions, brought us to life with Christ. . . .* (Eph 2:4-5)

Our Father is a God of great mercy and compassion. When we go to him in sorrow and contrition, he immediately grants us pardon and peace. At Mass we are reminded of his forgiving love, and we turn to him in earnest prayer. Immediately after the Lord's Prayer, in preparation for Holy Communion, we turn to him with our plea for mercy.

"Deliver us, Lord, from every evil, and grant us peace in our day, in your mercy keep us free from sin and protect us from all anxiety as we wait in joyful hope for the coming of our Savior, Jesus Christ."

In joy we respond: "For the kingdom, the power, and the glory are yours, now and forever."

10 *How shall I make a return to the LORD for all the good he has done for me? / The cup of salvation I will take up, / and I will call upon the name of the LORD.* (Ps 116:12-13)

Centuries before Jesus was incarnated into our world, the psalmist praised God for restoring him to good health. In gratitude, he took up the cup of sweet-smelling wine as an oblation to the Lord.

This verse is appropriately used in the liturgy as the prayer said by the priest before consuming the Precious Blood. The presence of Jesus under the appearance of wine heals us spiritually and restores our spiritual well-being.

Since all the faithful receive Holy Communion under both species, it is an ideal prayer for all communicants.

HOLY TRINITY

11 *"Holy, holy, holy is the Lord God almighty, who was, and who is, and who is to come."* (Rv 4:8)

The Preface of the Mass is an uplifting hymn of praise and thanksgiving offered to our triune God. It forms a transition from the Liturgy of the Word into the Liturgy of the Eucharist.

It usually begins with a prayer addressed to the Father, but also recalls the work of all three Divine Persons of the Trinity. We praise, thank, and glorify God for his tremendous blessings showered upon us. As we contemplate his boundless goodness, our hearts rejoice as did the four living creatures in the Book of Revelation. In the Mass we conclude the Preface with the liturgical prayer:

Holy, holy, holy Lord God of power and might,
heaven and earth are full of your glory.
Hosanna in the highest.
Blessed is he who comes in the name of the Lord.
Hosanna in the highest.

SON

12 *". . . Whatever you ask the Father in my name he may give you."* (Jn 15:16)

In the Eucharistic liturgy the church follows the directive Jesus encouraged by concluding the liturgical prayers in the name of Jesus. A variety of forms are used, but they all present a petition in Jesus' name.

To ask in the name of Jesus goes beyond mere words. It implies that we are striving to have the same dispositions which Jesus manifested, especially a lifestyle in conformity with the will of God. We ask with humility and trust, recognizing our total dependence on the Lord, keeping ourselves aware of the Father's unbounded love for us. When we strive to make our dispositions and attitudes the same as Jesus', we can be certain that our loving Father will respond graciously and generously to our prayer.

This we ask in Jesus' name.

13 *Then beginning with Moses and all the prophets, he interpreted to them what referred to him in all the scriptures.* (Lk 24:27)

Jesus' explanation of Scripture to the two disciples on the road to Emmaus is a model homily. It produced all the fruits for which a homily is intended.

The disciples were disappointed, discouraged, and depressed about the death of the Messiah. Jesus pointed out to them that all that Scripture had said about the Messiah was accurately fulfilled in what had happened. His interpretation opened their minds and hearts to understand the redemptive plan of God.

Like Jesus' words at Emmaus, the homily at Mass is intended to point out the hope, comfort, direction, peace, and joy which the Scriptures give us. May we say with the two disciples:

> "Were not our hearts burning [within us] while he spoke to us on the way and opened the scriptures to us?" (Lk 24:32)

14 *... "Rather, blessed are those who hear the word of God and observe it." (Lk 11:28)*

At every Mass we hear the priest or deacon announce: "A reading from the holy Gospel according to (N)," and at the end we rejoice in responding: "Praise to you, Lord Jesus Christ."

The message of the Gospel at Mass, like all of Scripture, is powerful and transforming. The words of the Gospel inspire and heal us, bring us comfort and joy. They can effect a conversion and transformation within us, if we permit them to find a home in our hearts.

The Gospel sets forth a rule of life. This is why Jesus said that those who hear the Word of God and keep it will indeed be blessed.

That is also why the Gospel is such an integral part of every Mass. May we live it every day.

15 *Jesus took bread, said the blessing, broke it, and giving it to his disciples said, "Take and eat; this is my body."* (Mt 26:26)

Notice the significance of the four verbs used in this passage of the Gospel.

Jesus *took:* Jesus accepts the gift of ourselves, symbolized by the bread, to offer us to the Father.

Jesus *blessed:* Jesus purifies and sanctifies us that we may enter into the presence of the Father as his children.

Jesus *broke:* The body of Jesus was broken on the cross in order to make the complete giving of himself on our behalf.

Jesus *gave:* Jesus gave himself totally to the Father as a perfect love offering to make up for our lack of love. He also gave himself to us to live with us and assist us in all that we do.

16 *Then he took a cup, gave thanks, and gave it to them, saying, "Drink from it, all of you, for this is my blood of the covenant, which will be shed on behalf of many for the forgiveness of sins."* (Mt 26:27-28)

Jesus changed wine into his own precious blood to signify his total giving of himself in atonement for our sins. In the Old Testament, the Lord reminds us that blood is the life of a living body and it should be placed on the altar so that atonement for sins may be made. "It is blood, as the seat of life, that makes atonement."

Jesus shed his very last drop of blood in reparation for our sins. St. John writes: "One soldier thrust his lance into his side, and immediately blood and water flowed out" (Jn 19:34).

In each Mass, Jesus offers himself anew in atonement for our sinfulness. Thank you, Lord Jesus.

17 ... *"Do this in memory of me."* (Lk 22:19)

Unfortunately there are many language barriers, especially in trying to translate ancient expressions into our modern idiom. "Memory" is such a word. We have no word which can convey exactly what Jesus meant when he said "Do this in memory of me." In order to comprehend his meaning, we must recall that God does not live in time and space as we do. He lives in the "eternal now."

In brief, the redemptive work of Jesus is still going on in the eternal now of God. When Jesus instituted the Eucharist, he entered into the "eternal now" of God, where everything is a reality and actuality now. When we offer the Eucharist we also enter into this "eternal now" and join all the angels and saints, all the people already baptized and those yet to be baptized in praising and glorifying God in this "mystery of faith."

This adds a much greater dimension to our act of worship.

18 *To the only God, our savior, through Jesus Christ our Lord be glory, majesty, power, and authority from ages past, now, and for ages to come. Amen.* (Jude 1:25)

The Mass is an act of worship which gives perfect honor and glory to God our almighty Father. We are painfully aware that our own act of worship is often distracted and often made only half-heartedly.

In celebrating the Eucharist, we are privileged to offer our worship, adoration, thanks, and praise to the Father through Jesus our eternal high priest in union with the Holy Spirit.

At the close of the Eucharistic Prayer we

pause to express our offering in this dox-
ology:

Through him, with him, in him, in the
unity of the Holy Spirit all glory and honor
is yours, almighty Father forever and ever.
Amen.

19 ... *"Behold, the Lamb of God, who takes away the sin of the world."* (Jn 1:29)

The sacrificial death of Jesus was pre-
figured by the Passover Lamb. Jesus offered
the gift of himself as a perfect love-offering
to the Father to make up for the love which
our sinfulness has denied him. Sin is a
refusal to love. By offering his life as the
Lamb of God, Jesus made an infinite act of
love to the Father in our name.

As we approach the solemn moment of
Communion at Mass, we are reminded of
the redeeming love of Jesus and the many
blessings he is bringing us in Holy Communion. The words of the liturgy are fitting
reminder:

Happy are those who are called to his
supper.

20 ... *"Lord, I am not worthy to have you enter under my roof; only say the word and my servant will be healed."* (Mt 8:8)

These edifying words of the centurion
were immortalized by the church when they

were introduced into the Communion Rite at Mass. Jews are forbidden to go into the homes of Gentiles, but this was not the only reason for the centurion's word to Jesus. His was a firm faith which assured him that distance was no problem for the divine healing power of Jesus.

How fittingly these words remind us of the tremendous privilege which is ours as we approach Jesus in Holy Communion. The awareness of our unworthiness disposes us to the influence of God's grace.

"Lord, I am not worthy to receive you, but only say the word and I shall be healed."

HOLY SPIRIT

21 *Exalted at the right hand of God, he received the promise of the holy Spirit from the Father and poured it forth, as you [both] see and hear.* (Acts 2:33)

The Eucharistic celebration is a sublime Trinitarian prayer. All three persons of the Blessed Trinity are praised, honored, and adored in this unique act of worship. All three are implored for the special assistance we need.

When Jesus fulfilled the Father's plan by completing his mission as Redeemer, the Holy Spirit was enabled to operate in our lives to purify and sanctify us and bring to us fruits of this redemption.

In each Mass we offer him ourselves that he may enrich, purify, and sanctify us as we journey through this land of exile to our heavenly home.

22 *He [Simeon] came in the Spirit into the temple; and when the parents brought in the child Jesus to perform the custom of the law in regard to him, he took him into his arms and blessed God. . . .* (Lk 2:27-28)

Enlightened by the Holy Spirit, Simeon recognized the Messiah in this little infant. Elizabeth, likewise, recognized the unborn Jesus in his mother's womb. This was the gift of the Holy Spirit.

At Mass, we pray that the same Holy Spirit will enlighten us to appreciate the presence of Jesus hidden under the appearances of bread and wine. We ask that these gifts may become *for us* the body and blood of our Lord Jesus. They will certainly become Christ's body and blood, but will we be able to be totally aware of his divine presence? Hence we pray:

Let your Spirit come upon these gifts to make them holy so that they may become *for us* the body and blood of our Lord Jesus Christ. (EP II, emphasis mine)

23 *Thus faith comes from what is heard, and what is heard comes through the word of Christ.* (Rom 10:17)

After we hear the Scriptures read at Mass and a homily amplifying their message, we renew our belief in all the Lord has revealed. Together with our brothers and sisters worshiping with us, we make a formal profession of faith. This verbalization of all that we believe in enlivens our own faith. We proclaim among other tenets:

> We believe in the Holy Spirit, the Lord, the giver of life, who proceeds from the Father and the Son. With the Father and the Son he is worshiped and glorified.

This profession not only renews our faith, but it keeps us aware of the power of the Holy Spirit operative in our lives and keeps us open to and cooperative with his inspirations and influence.

Thank you, Holy Spirit, for our gift of faith.

24 *"And [behold] I am sending the promise of my Father upon you; but stay in the city until you are clothed with power from on high."*
(Lk 24:49)

In the Eucharistic celebration, the Lord has devised a privileged means for us to bring the gift of ourselves and all that we do to present it to the Father along with the gift of himself. Our gifts are symbolized by the bread and wine which adequately represent us since they represent the necessities of life—food and drink.

Since the gift of ourselves may be given half-heartedly or even reluctantly, we pray that the Holy Spirit may sanctify them before they are united with the gift of Jesus.

And so Father, we bring you these gifts. We ask you to make them holy by the power of your Spirit, that they may become the body and blood of your Son, our Lord Jesus Christ, at whose command we celebrate this Eucharist. (EP III)

25 *This is how we know that we remain in him and he in us, that he has given us of his Spirit.* (1 Jn 4:13)

We are living with the risen Jesus and he with us as well as with the people we meet each day. Amid the countless duties and distractions of the day, we easily become oblivious of his abiding presence in us and others.

The Eucharist is a unifying sacrament binding us together in a Christian community. Since the Holy Spirit is the builder of community, at Mass we pray:

Lord, look upon this sacrifice which you have given to your church; and by your Holy Spirit, gather all who share this one bread and one cup into one body of Christ living sacrifice of praise. (EP IV)

In the Mass our own soft voices become a thunderous chorus of praise, as we unite with all the members of Christ's body and offer our praise to God.

26 *While they were worshiping the Lord and fasting, the holy Spirit said, "Set apart for me Barnabas and Saul for the work to which I have called them."* (Acts 13:2)

The Holy Spirit's inspiration, guidance, and direction is quite evident in the work of evangelization. His divine influence comes to us directly through many and varied channels. It was during the liturgy that he directed Paul and Barnabas to continue their apostolate among the Gentiles.

In Eucharistic Prayer III, we pray that his divine indwelling may unite us that we may become one body and that we may draw many others into the body of Christ.

Grant that we, who are nourished by his body and blood, may be filled with his Holy Spirit and become one body, one spirit in Christ. (EP III)

27 *How much more will the ministry of the Spirit be glorious? For if the ministry of condemnation was glorious, the ministry of righteousness will abound much more in glory.*
(2 Cor 3:8-9)

The ministry of the Holy Spirit is our sanctification. At baptism he came to make his temple within us. He endows us with his gifts and graces. He aids us in times of stress and strain, in disappointment and discouragement, in temptation and trial.

We begin Eucharistic Prayer III by praising the Father for his holiness which comes to us through his Son, but primarily through the ministry of the Holy Spirit. Let us pray:

Father, you are holy indeed, and all creation rightly gives you praise. All life, all holiness comes from you through your Son, Jesus Christ our Lord, by the working of the Holy Spirit. (EP III)

28 *In him you also, who have heard the word of truth, the gospel of your salvation, and have believed in him, were sealed with the promised holy Spirit.* (Eph 1:13)

Jesus promised to send us the Holy Spirit who would teach us everything and remind us of all that he taught us. In order that he might complete the work of sanctification in us, the Holy Spirit makes of us his special temple, dwelling with us and within us.

By his presence, the Spirit helps us keep our vision fixed heavenward above all the enticements of our modern world.

He gives us hope and courage in trials and difficulties. He fills us with his peace and joy as he pours out his love upon us. That we may be open to his divine influence we pray at Mass:

And that we might live no longer for
ourselves but for him, he sent the Holy
Spirit from you, Father, as the first gift to
those who believe, to complete his work
on earth and bring us the fullness of
grace. (EP IV)

29 *. . . The bread that we break, is it not a
participation in the body of Christ?
Because the loaf of bread is one, we, though many,
are one body, for we all partake of the one loaf.*
(1 Cor 10:16-17)

The Holy Eucharist is the sacrament of
Christian unity. Jesus comes to us to unite us
to himself as members of his body, pro-
fessing the same faith and journeying on the
same walk of life.

The Holy Spirit is the builder of Christian
community. Genuine community is built
not so much on rules and regulations, but on
the love we have for God, for ourselves, and
for our neighbors. The Spirit is the source of
divine love, and we call upon him during the
Eucharist to fill us with his divine love.

May all of you who share in the body and
blood of Christ, be brought together in
unity by the Holy Spirit. (EP II)

30 . . . *"Your light must shine before others, that they may see your good deeds and glorify your heavenly Father."* (Mt 5:16)

We are greatly enriched with the Lord's divine life and love each time we are privileged to offer the Eucharist. Replenished with his love, peace, and joy, the Lord invites us to "let our light shine before others." We are certainly aware that we cannot accomplish this mission alone.

At this stage in the liturgy, the Lord imparts to us the special blessing of the Father, Son, and Holy Spirit to equip us for our mission. A blessing is a gift, and the chief gift we receive here is the Holy Spirit who guides, encourages, and strengthens us for our daily apostolate.

With open hands, minds, and hearts let us receive his blessing as the celebrant prays at the end of Mass:

May almighty God bless you, the Father, and the Son, and the Holy Spirit.

HOLY TRINITY

31 *"Go, therefore, and make disciples of all nations, baptizing them in the name of the Father, and of the Son, and of the holy Spirit, teaching them to observe all that I have commanded you. . . ."* (Mt 28:19-20)

With these words, Jesus commissioned every one of us to make him better known and loved throughout the world. When we offer the Eucharist with Jesus, we are better equipped to reflect his love, peace, and joy to everyone we meet.

Each one of the dismissals at Mass is in reality an invitation to fulfill this commission of making Jesus better known by reflecting his mind and heart in all we say and do. Jesus became Eucharist for us, now we are to become Eucharist to others.

"Go in the peace of Christ." / "The Mass is ended, go in peace." / "Go in peace to love and serve the Lord."

And we do not go alone, because the Lord goes with us.

Glory be to the Father,
and to the Son,
and to the Holy Spirit.

Index of Scriptures

Scriptural passages introducing the theme and prayer for each day. Other Scriptures found in the commentary are not listed here.

1 Kings

Passage	Month	Day
8:50	6	3

2 Chronicles

Passage	Month	Day
6:27	6	8

Nehemiah

Passage	Month	Day
9:20	1	22

Judith

Passage	Month	Day
9:11	1	6
16:14	4	23

Tobit

Passage	Month	Day
12:14	7	8

2 Maccabees

Passage	Month	Day
7:20	9	9
7:22-23	4	6

Job

Passage	Month	Day
33:4	4	24

Psalms

Passage	Month	Day
16:11	1	4
18:2-3	1	7
19:2	4	8
23:1-2	1	9
24:1-2	4	7
25:3	8	7
31:25	9	3
33:4	8	9
33:21-22	9	1
33:22	9	5
34:5-6	10	1
36:6	5	9
37:11	11	6
41:5	7	6
42:12	9	7
43:4	10	4
45:3	1	15
50:23	12	6
51:12-13	6	24
51:14	10	7
57:11-12	5	3
69:17	6	7
72:2-3	1	16
103:1, 3-4	7	4
107:20-21	7	2
110:4	1	17
116:12-13	12	10
119:165	11	3

Isaiah (continued)

Passage	Month	Day
54:10	11	8
61:1	7	31
61:10	10	9

Baruch

Passage	Month	Day
4:22	10	3

Ezekiel

Passage	Month	Day
11:19-20	1	29
18:23	6	6
34:15-16	7	9
37:26	11	2

Hosea

Passage	Month	Day
11:4	7	5
12:7	9	6

Joel

Passage	Month	Day
3:1-2	1	30

Micah

Passage	Month	Day
5:3-4	11	11
7:7	9	8

Zechariah

Passage	Month	Day
9:9	1	18
12:1	1	21

Malachi

Passage	Month	Day
2:10	8	8

Matthew

Passage	Month	Day
2:2	2	11
2:2	8	11
3:11	7	23
3:16-17	2	31
5:9	11	14
5:16	12	30
6:9-10	12	7
6:14-15	6	17
6:26	2	1
6:30	5	6
6:32-33	2	2
7:11	2	3
8:8	12	20
8:10	8	17
9:13	6	15
10:7-8	5	14
11:4-5	7	11
11:25	2	6
11:29	2	17

Luke (continued)

Passage	Month	Day
22:19	12	17
22:19-20	4	20
22:32	8	19
22:51	7	19
23:34	6	19
23:43	6	20
24:25	8	20
24:27	12	13
24:41	10	18
24:49	12	24
24:52	10	19

John

Passage	Month	Day
1:3-4	4	11
1:10	4	12
1:14	4	13
1:29	12	19
1:32	2	24
1:36	2	13
3:16	6	10
4:10	4	17
4:14	4	16
4:23	6	22
5:6	7	16
6:11	5	16

John (continued)

Passage	Month	Day
6:29	8	15
6:35	2	18
6:63	4	26
7:37-38	5	12
8:11	6	13
8:12	2	15
10:11	2	16
10:14-15	6	11
10:17-18	5	18
10:29	2	7
10:38	8	16
11:21, 23-24	9	16
11:25-26	8	18
13:15	5	11
13:34	5	13
14:1	8	1
14:6	2	14
14:16-17	2	28
14:23	2	4
14:26	2	29
14:26	7	30
14:27	11	17
15:1-2	2	8
15:11	10	15
15:13	5	15
15:16	12	12
16:7	5	21

1 Corinthians (cont.)

Passage	Month	Day
12:11	5	26
12:13	4	29
12:26	10	27
13:6	10	26
13:7	9	25

Galatians

Passage	Month	Day
4:6	3	7
5:5	8	30
5:5	9	30
5:16	6	29
5:22	10	23
5:22-23	11	22

2 Corinthians

Passage	Month	Day
1:3-4	9	10
1:7	9	24
1:21-22	4	31
3:8-9	12	27
3:12	9	23
3:17	6	21
4:13	8	23
5:1	5	10
5:5	8	29
6:16	3	2
6:16	3	9
6:18	3	6
9:15	5	24
13:11	11	26
13:13	12	1

Ephesians

Passage	Month	Day
1:7	6	14
1:11-12	9	15
1:13	12	28
1:17	3	8
1:18	9	21
2:4-5	12	9
2:8	8	28
2:17-18	11	21
2:22	4	28
3:14-19	8	31
3:16	8	22
3:16-17	9	22
4:6	3	5
4:30	3	25
5:18, 20	3	31
6:16-17	8	27
6:18	10	24

James

Passage	Month	Day
1:17	3	4
2:21-22	8	3
3:18	11	23
4:6	5	5

1 Peter

Passage	Month	Day
1:2	11	31
1:8-9	10	20
1:18-19	6	25
2:5	3	17
2:24	7	20
4:14	3	28

2 Peter

Passage	Month	Day
1:21	3	27

1 John

Passage	Month	Day
1:7	3	20
2:25	4	19
3:1	3	3
3:24	3	29
4:2	11	25
4:13	12	25
4:15	3	11
5:14	9	20

Jude

Passage	Month	Day
1:2	11	24
1:25	12	18

Revelation

Passage	Month	Day
4:8	12	11
4:11	4	10
7:17	3	13
19:7	10	30
21:6	4	30
22:16	3	16
22:17	5	30